Study Guide

American Government and Politics Today: The Essentials

2009–2010 EDITION

Barbara A. Bardes

Mack C. Shelley

Steffen w. Schmidt

Prepared by

Stephen Mergner

Georgetown College

Australia • Brazil • Japan • Korea • Mexico • Singapore • Spain • United Kingdom • United States

ISBN-13: 978-0-495-57238-1
ISBN-10: 0-495-57238-1

Wadsworth
20 Channel Center
Boston, MA 02210
USA

Cengage Learning is a leading provider of customized learning solutions with office locations around the globe, including Singapore, the United Kingdom, Australia, Mexico, Brazil, and Japan. Locate your local office at: **international.cengage.com/region**

Cengage Learning products are represented in Canada by Nelson Education, Ltd.

For your course and learning solutions, visit **academic.cengage.com**

Purchase any of our products at your local college store or at our preferred online store **www.ichapters.com**

Printed in the United States of America
1 2 3 4 5 6 7 12 11 10 09

Table of Contents

Chapter 1
THE DEMOCRATIC REPUBLIC

CHAPTER SUMMARY

Politics is the "great game" that resolves conflict and determines the people who receive benefits and privileges. Two fundamental principles that guide these benefits are order and liberty. Through changes in the democratic process, the American political system evolves. This chapter will discuss some of the questions and principles that are fundamental to the American political system.

Politics and Government

Politics is defined by Harold Lasswell as the process of resolving conflict and deciding "who gets what, when, and how" in a society. More specifically, politics can be seen as the operations of conflict and processes of conflict resolution in society. Conflict is always present in society, for three major reasons: the differences in belief or ideology, the differences in the perceived goals of the society, and the fact that scarce resources exist and not every want can be satisfied by society. Government is the preeminent institution making decisions and establishing political values.

Why is Government Necessary?

The situation in Somalia since 1991 and the current situation in Iraq show the importance of the government's role in providing order for normal life to exist. Order must be tempered with liberty for democratic values to exist. An institution requires authority, legitimacy, and power in order to accomplish its purpose. Authority is the feature of a leader or institution that compels obedience. Usually this obedience comes from legitimacy. Legitimacy is the status conferred by the people on the officials, acts, and institutions of the government. Power is the ability to cause others to modify their behavior and to conform to what the power holder wants. To sum up, authority is the legal use of power.

Democracy and Other Forms of Government

A fundamental question of politics has to do with who makes political decisions for a society. Totalitarianism is a government in which a small group or a single individual makes all political decisions for the society. Authoritarianism differs from totalitarianism only in that the former system has social and economic institutions that are not under the complete control of the ruler or ruling party. Aristocracy refers to a system in which decisions are made by the "best suited" in terms of wealth, education, intelligence, and family prestige. Theocracy is a form of government in which the rule of law is believed to be driven by God or the gods. In practice, it is rule by religious leaders who are typically self-appointed. In a democracy, the majority of people make decisions and rule is based on the consent of the people. Direct democracy is people making decisions in person rather than through elected leaders, as in the model of the New England town meeting. A possible danger of this form of democracy is mob rule, in which the majority abuses the rights of minority groups. This danger has led our society to create a democratic republic, in which representatives are elected by the people to make and enforce laws and policies. The three principles essential for democratic government in our society are universal suffrage, the right of all adults to vote for representatives; majority rule with the protection of minority rights; and limited government, the authority of government limited by a written document or widely held beliefs.

What Kind of Democracy Do We Have?

Majoritarianism holds that a democratic government ought to act in line with the desires of the majority of the people. This is sometimes considered a poor description of the American system due to low voter turnout and poorly informed voters. Elite theory has suggested that society is ruled by a small number of wealthy people who exercise power in their self-interest. The primary goal of such a society is stability because elites do not want to see any change in their status. The elite can be maintained and recruited through the educational system. Pluralism theory has proposed that conflict in society occurs among interest groups. Bargaining and compromise among groups determine political decision-making. It has been suggested, however, that interest groups can become so powerful that the society is virtually paralyzed by the struggle among them. Experts contend that aspects of all three systems are present in the American model of democracy.

Fundamental Values

Political culture can be defined as a patterned set of ideas, values, and ways of thinking about government and politics. The process by which political beliefs and values are transmitted to new immigrants and to our children is called political socialization. The fundamental values of American political culture can be defined as follows: liberty, the greatest freedom of individuals that is consistent with the freedom of other individuals in society; equality, the belief that all people are of equal worth; and property, the right of individual ownership. In some senses and cases, liberty and equality can be in conflict, as can the ideals of property and equality. Political culture has been important in holding society together by persuading people to support the existing political process even in the face of such conflicts.

Political Ideologies

Ideology can be defined as a comprehensive and logical set of beliefs about the nature of people as well as the institutions and role of government. American beliefs have been dominated by two moderate ideologies. Liberalism is the belief that includes support of positive government action to improve the welfare of individuals, support for civil rights, and support for political and social change. Conservatism is the belief that includes support of a limited role for government's helping individuals, support for traditional values, and a cautious response to change. The four-cornered grid provides a more sophisticated view of four possible ideologies (see Figure 1-1). Totalitarian ideologies have provided the major challenge to American values, with the latest example being Islamic totalitarianism.

A Republic, If You Can Keep It

A republic is one of the most challenging forms of government to maintain as citizen participation is an essential element of its long-term legitimacy. Since 2001, a majority of Americans do not trust government to do what is right or that "things have pretty seriously gotten off on the wrong track." In another poll a majority of Americans believe that "the government does not listen to people like me." This erosion of public support could potentially threaten the legitimacy of our republic. Since 2001, government has grown at an unprecedented rate, both in money spent and departmental growth. Of particular interest is a strengthening of the executive branch's power under the current administration. This expansion of power has largely remained unchecked by either the Congress or the Courts.

KEY TERMS

anarchy
aristocracy
authoritarianism
authority
Bill of Rights
capitalism
civil liberties
communism
consent of the people
conservatism
democracy
democratic republic
direct democracy
dominant culture
elite theory
equality
fascism

government
ideology
initiative
institution
Islamism
legislature
legitimacy
liberalism
libertarianism
liberty
limited government
majoritarianism
majority
majority rule
oligarchy
order
pluralism

political culture
political socialization
politics
popular sovereignty
property
recall
referendum

representative
republic
socialism
theocracy
totalitarian regime
universal suffrage

OTHER RESOURCES

A number of valuable supplements are available to students using the Schmidt, Shelley, and Bardes text. A list of suggested supplements is at the end of the chapter. Ask your instructor how to obtain these resources. One supplement is highlighted here, E-mocracy.

E-MOCRACY EXERCISES

Direct URL: http://www.theadvocates.org/quizp/index.html

Surfing Instructions:
Log on to www.politicalscience.wadsworth.com/amgov
On the left side, click on "Government Foundations."
On the left side, place your cursor upon "ideologies."
In the "ideologies" drop-down menu select "Internet activities."
Select the link to the #2 "World's Smallest Political Quiz" and see how it categorizes your personal political ideology.

Study Questions
1. Are the quiz's results what you expected?
2. Is your ideology the same as that of your parents?
3. Why do you think this is so?
4. What information from this chapter can help you understand how the development of your personal ideology was formed?

PRACTICE EXAM
(Answers appear at the end of this chapter.)

Fill-in-the-Blank   Supply the missing word(s) or term(s) to complete the sentence.

1. All major definitions of politics try to explain how human beings resolve _____ and decide "who gets what, when and how" in their society.

2. The features of a leader or an institution that compel obedience are called _____.

3. The ancient Greek city-state of Athens is often considered to be the historical model for _____ _____.

4. The U.S. Constitution creates a form of republican government known as a _____ _____.

5. From the elite theory perspective, new members of the elite are recruited through the _____ _____.

6. In the pluralist's view, politics is the struggle among _____ _____ to gain benefits for their members.

7. A fundamental source of political socialization is the _____.

8. Democracy, liberty, equality, and property lie at the core of American _____ _____.

9. Since 2001, _____ _____ is the form of totalitarianism that most threatens our country's interests.

10. Within the American electorate, the two ideological viewpoints that are most commonly held are _____ and _____.

True/False   Circle the appropriate letter to indicate if the statement is true or false.

T   F   1. Political scientists agree that politics involves the resolution of social conflict.

T   F   2. In democratic nations, most citizens comply with the law because they accept the authority of the government and its officials.

T   F   3. Direct democracy in ancient Athens allowed all people to participate in the governing process.

T   F   4. James Madison was a strong advocate of a "pure democracy" for the American political system.

T   F   5. In a Democratic Republic, the people hold the ultimate power over the government through the election process.

T   F   6. The elite perspective sees the mass population as active and involved in the decisions of government.

T   F   7. A democratic system can be paralyzed by the struggle among interest groups.

T   F   8. The basic guarantee of liberties for citizens within the American political system is called egalitarianism.

T   F   9. Totalitarianism continues to be a major threat to the United States.

T   F   10. American's trust in government has been declining rapidly since 2001.

Multiple choice   Circle the correct response.

1. All definitions of politics try to explain how human beings regulate
    a. natural resources within their society.
    b. good and evil within a complex society.
    c. self-expression.
    d. conflict within their society.
    e. economic equality.

2. A form of government in which every aspect of political, social, and economic life is controlled by the government is called a(n)
    a. democratic regime.
    b. socialist regime.
    c. totalitarian regime.
    d. oligarchy.
    e. dominant culture.

3. The New England Town Meeting would most closely fit which of the following?
    a. direct democracy
    b. the aristocracy
    c. representative democracy
    d. democratic republic
    e. pluralism

4. The Athenian model of government was considered
    a. the purest model for direct democracy.
    b. a weak and ineffective form of government.
    c. the reason the Roman legions were able to conquer Greece.
    d. the forerunner of communism.
    e. the forerunner of socialism.

5. Initiative is a procedure by which voters can
    a. directly make laws.
    b. remove elected officials.
    c. propose a law or constitutional amendment.
    d. place candidates on a ballot.
    e. vote online.

6. The U.S. Constitution creates a form of republican government known as a
    a. pure democracy.
    b. confederation.
    c. Democratic Republic.
    d. majoritarian system.
    e. direct democracy.

7. A central feature to the American governmental system is
    a. the supremacy of Congress over the other branches.
    b. control of the airwaves.
    c. the tendency to provide foreign aid to every country.
    d. equality of every individual before the law.
    e. majority rule.

8. To ensure that majority rule does not become oppressive, modern democracies
    a. provide guarantees of minority rights.
    b. have constitutions that are difficult to amend.
    c. use plurality voting for most decisions.
    d. use affirmative action programs.
    e. hold free, competitive elections.

9. The U.S. Constitution
    a. does not set forth enough detail as to how the government should function.
    b. is too open to interpretation, which creates confusion for government leaders.
    c. has more amendments than any other national constitution.
    d. sets forth the fundamental structure of the government and the limits to its power.
    e. requires a majority vote to elect all officials.

10. According to the elite theory,
    a. society is ruled by a small number of people who exercise power to further their self-interest.
    b. the elite cannot be corrupted because they have so much wealth already.
    c. the elite know what is best for the poor.
    d. the elite know how to negotiate better than others.
    e. the government is always the elite.

11. Pluralist theory believes that decisions are made in American politics by
    a. the mass population.
    b. the governing elites.
    c. the wealthy.
    d. the competition between groups trying to gain benefits for their members.
    e. the political parties.

12. The pattern set of ideas, values, and ways of thinking about government and politics is referred to as
    a.   public opinion.
    b.   democratic heritage.
    c.   political culture.
    d.   consensus of opinion.
    e.   majority opinion.

13. The process by which political beliefs and values are transmitted to new immigrants and to our children is called
    a.   enculturation.
    b.   education.
    c.   political socialization.
    d.   propaganda.
    e.   dominant culture.

14. Democracy, liberty, equality, and property are
    a.   concepts that no longer have meaning in modern political systems.
    b.   now thought to be unattainable in a modern pluralistic society.
    c.   concepts that lie at the core of American political culture.
    d.   concepts that encompass our entire political heritage.
    e.   now thought to be impossible to achieve since the events of September 11, 2001.

15. The ideology that believes the government should exercise the least power is
    a.   socialism.
    b.   liberalism.
    c.   conservatism.
    d.   libertarianism.
    e.   totalitarianism.

16. Communism and fascism are examples of which ideology?
    a.   socialism
    b.   guided democracy
    c.   libertarianism
    d.   liberalism
    e.   totalitarianism

17. In 2007, what percentage of American's trusted the government to do what is right?
    a.   0% of the population.
    b.   24% of the population.
    c.   56% of the population.
    d.   88% of the population.
    e.   100% of the population.

18. Which branch of government has experienced the most growth since 2001?
    a.   Executive
    b.   Legislative
    c.   Judiciary
    d.   State
    e.   Local

19. _____ is the political philosophy that maintains a strong skepticism towards most government activities.
    a. Communism.
    b. Liberalism.
    c. Islamism.
    d. Socialism.
    e. Libertarianism.

20. Which of the following forms of totalitarianism is the most current threat to US interests?
    a. Communism.
    b. Fascism.
    c. Islamism.
    d. Capitalism.
    e. Libertarianism.

Short Essay   Briefly address the major concepts raised by the following questions:

1. Explain the role of politics and government in an organized society.

2. Explain the origins of democracy and the different types of democracy.

3. Define the fundamental elements of the American political culture.

4. Compare and contrast the concepts of liberalism and conservatism.

ANSWERS TO THE PRACTICE EXAM

Fill-in-the-Blank

1. conflict
2. authority
3. direct democracy
4. democratic republic
5. educational system
6. interest groups
7. family
8. political culture
9. Islamic Fundamentalism
10. liberalism, conservatism

True/False

1. T	3. F	5. T	7. T	9. T
2. T	4. F	6. F	8. F	10. T

Multiple Choice

1. d	6. c	11. d	16. e
2. c	7. d	12. c	17. c
3. a	8. a	13. c	18. a
4. a	9. d	14. c	19. e
5. c	10. a	15. d	20. c

Short Essay

An adequate short answer consists of several paragraphs that relate to concepts addressed by the question. Always demonstrate your knowledge of the ideas by giving examples. The following represent major ideas that should be included in the short essay answer.

1. Explain the role of politics and government in an organized society.

Definitions of politics—Harold Lasswell, the process of resolving conflicts and deciding "who gets what, when, and how."
Government is the preeminent institution that make decisions that resolve conflicts and give benefits.
Government is necessary to keep order and protect rights by using authority and legitimacy.

2. Explain the origins of democracy and the different types of democracy.

Athenian model of direct democracy—every citizen has a responsibility to participate through initiative, referendum, and recall.
Democratic republic—a republic in which the people vote for representatives to make laws and other decisions for the people.
Principles of western representative democracy—the emphasis on elected officials making all policy decisions.
Constitutional democracy—limited government; that is, the power of government is limited by a written document or constitution.

3. Define the fundamental elements of the American political culture.

- Liberty—The greatest freedom of individuals that is consistent with the freedom of other individuals in society. Freedom of speech and freedom of religion are good examples. Freedom can be restricted in a time of national emergency.
- Equality—The concept that all people are of equal worth. The meaning of this concept is often debated. Does it mean equal political status or equal opportunity?
- Property—It can be seen as giving its owner political power and the liberty to do whatever he or she wants.
  These are the three core values often linked with majority rule.

4. Compare and contrast the concepts of liberalism and conservatism.

- Ideology is a set of ideas about the goal of politics.
- Liberalism represents:
  - Positive government action to solve social problems
  - Advocacy for civil rights
  - Advocacy for social change
- Conservatism represents:
  - Faith in the private sector to solve most social problems
  - Advocacy of individuals' actions to protect their rights
  - Advocacy for a return to traditional values

Chapter 2
THE CONSTITUTION

CHAPTER SUMMARY
The story of the creation of the Constitution is told in each generation and is the key to understanding American government and politics.

The Colonial Background
Jamestown, Virginia, founded in 1607, was the first British settlement in North America that endured, albeit with difficulty through a "starving time" possibly brought about by a drought. Plymouth, Massachusetts followed in 1620 and was founded by a group of religious Separatists sailing from England on the *Mayflower*. They were responsible for the Mayflower Compact and its pledge of the people's consent to live under the rule of law. Additional settlements established by both the English government and immigrants from Britain followed in Massachusetts and Connecticut. (See the Milestones in Early U.S. Political History.)

British Restrictions and Colonial Grievances
Until the 1760s, the colonies enjoyed a large measure of autonomy from the British crown. Under King George III, the British government decided to tax the colonists to pay for the French and Indian War expenses. The Sugar Act in 1764, Stamp Act in 1765, and a suite of duties levied in 1767 led to the Boston Tea Party, which caused the British Parliament to pass The Coercive (or Intolerable) Acts in 1774.

The Colonial Response: The Continental Congresses
The colonists responded to the British with the First Continental Congress held in 1774, which issued a petition of grievances and attempted to create committees to bring the colonists together. The Second Continental Congress met in 1775, when fighting had already occurred between the colonists and the British. The Second Congress established an army with George Washington as commander-in-chief. The public was won over by the hugely influential *Common Sense*, by Thomas Paine. In this work, Paine presented an argument regarding the need for a declaration of independence from Britain.

Declaring Independence
In early 1776, the Second Continental Congress approved the Resolution of Independence to establish legitimacy and to seek foreign military aid. The Second Congress assigned Thomas Jefferson the task of writing a formal declaration of independence. This Declaration of Independence was approved on July 4, 1776, and contained three major principles, based on the ideas of English political philosopher John Locke: natural (or "inalienable") rights, consent of the governed, and the right to change the government. The fighting continued for five more years, ending in 1781. In 1783, the British government formally recognized that the United States was an independent body.

The Articles of Confederation: Our First Form of Government
In 1781, the Articles of Confederation, a voluntary association of independent states, was created. (See Figure 2-1 and Table 2-1 for information on the powers of this form of government.) The articles represented real cooperation among the thirteen American states, but the lack of taxing authority made them too weak a form of government to survive. Shay's Rebellion in 1786 spurred political leaders to take action to change the Articles.

Drafting the Constitution
The Annapolis Convention was called in 1786 to discuss the weaknesses of the national government. At this meeting, a call was sent out for all of the states to attend a general convention in Philadelphia in May 1787. Fifty-five delegates, representing every state (except Rhode Island), attended the Philadelphia convention. The delegates were mostly nationalists, but included monarchists, democratic nationalists, non-democratic

nationalists, and some strong state government advocates. The debates, which began the first day, produced two major plans: the Virginia Plan, which proposed an entirely new national government, favoring large states; and the New Jersey Plan, which was essentially an amendment to the Articles of Confederation. The "Great Compromise," brokered by the Connecticut delegation, broke the deadlock between advocates of the two proposals. This compromise called for a bicameral legislature as a new form of national government. Slavery and other issues between the agrarian South and the mercantile North were resolved by other compromises, including the Three-Fifths Compromise and a promise that exports would not be subject to taxation. Although most historians believe that this compromise on slavery was necessary in order to achieve unity, some argue that an opportunity for an outright ban was missed. The final agreement included separation of powers (sometimes known at the Madisonian model), a system of checks and balances, and an Electoral College to elect the president. (See Figure 2-2 for a view of the system of checks and balances.)

The Final Document

Thirty-nine delegates approved the Constitution on September 17, 1787. The document established five fundamental principles: popular sovereignty, a republican form of government, limited government, separation of powers, and a federal system allowing for broad states' rights.

The Difficult Road to Ratification

The opposing forces in the battle for ratification were the Federalists, who were in favor of ratification, and the Anti-Federalists, who were opposed to ratifying the Constitution as it was drafted. Alexander Hamilton, James Madison, and John Jay wrote the *Federalist Papers*, which were influential in the success of the ratification effort. In 1788, New Hampshire became the ninth state to ratify the Constitution, thus allowing it to be formally established. (See Table 2-2 for the ratification vote in each of the thirteen original states.) Popular support for the Constitution at the time has been the subject of debate, especially from Charles Beard. He believed that wealthy property owners were behind the Constitution and that a majority of Americans did not support it.

The Bill of Rights

Ratification of the Constitution was probably dependent upon the Federalists' promises of amendments to the Constitution to protect individual liberties. James Madison culled through state convention recommendations to produce what became the Bill of Rights. The ten amendments of the Bill of Rights were ratified in 1791, though without what Madison considered the most important amendment, one that would limit the power of states over their citizens.

Altering the Constitution: The Formal Amendment Process

Amending the Constitution is a purposefully rigorous two-step process. The first step is to propose a new amendment. This can be done by either a two-thirds vote in both houses of Congress or by a national convention called by Congress at the request of two-thirds of the states. The second step in amending the Constitution is to ratify the amendment. Ratification is accomplished by either a three-fourths vote of the state legislatures or by a three-fourths vote of state conventions called to ratify the amendment. (See Figure 2-3.) Congress has considered more than 11,000 amendments, of which 33 have been submitted for ratification, and only 27 have been ratified. (See Table 2-3.) Since 1919, most proposed amendments have had a seven-year ratification limit, but the Twentieth-Seventh Amendment, ratified in 1992, took 203 years.

Informal Methods of Constitutional Change

While there have been few formal amendments to the Constitution over the centuries, informal change has occurred on a more frequent basis. These informal changes include those made by legislation passed by Congress under the commerce clause and Article III, Section 1 of the Constitution. The Constitution has also changed through the creation of executive agreements by presidents to conduct foreign policy or executive orders in his handling of the federal bureaucracy. Additionally, the Supreme Court claimed the power of judicial review in the case of *Marbury v. Madison* (1803). Through interpretation, custom, and tradition, the Constitution's extensive use in day-to-day government activities has influenced its meaning.

KEY TERMS

Anti-Federalist
bicameral legislature
checks and balances
confederation
Electoral College
executive agreement
executive order
federal system
Federalist
Great Compromise
judicial review

Madisonian model
natural rights
ratification
representative assembly
separation of powers
social contract
state
supremacy doctrine
unicameral legislature

OTHER RESOURCES

A number of valuable supplements are available to students using the Schmidt, Shelley, and Bardes text. A list of suggested supplements is at the end of the chapter. Ask your instructor how to obtain these resources. One supplement is highlighted here, findlaw.com.

E-MOCRACY EXERCISES

Direct URL: (Ohio in this case) http://www.legislature.state.oh.us/constitution.cfm?Part=1

Surfing Instructions:
Log on to www.findlaw.com/casecode/state.html
Choose a state from the list
Under "State Resources," select "constitution" to view the state's constitution.
Select "Bill of Rights" from your constitutional categories.
Please read your state's Bill of Rights and compare your state's rights to your federal rights.

Study Questions
1. Does your state provide more or less rights than the federal government?

2. What rights does the state provide that the federal government does not? Why do you think this is so?

3. Please compare this state's Bill of Rights to that of another state. What patterns and differences to you see? What could account for these similarities and variances?

PRACTICE EXAM
(Answers appear at the end of this chapter.)

Fill-in-the-Blank   Supply the missing word(s) or term(s) to complete the sentence.

1. The passage of the Coercive Acts by the British Parliament was in response to the _____ ____ _____.

2. The rights of "life, liberty, and the pursuit of happiness" are referred to as _____ _____.

3. A voluntary association of independent states is referred to as a(n)_____.

4. The plan of government that introduced the idea of a bicameral legislature was the _____ _____.

5. The agreement that resolved the differences between the large and small states over representation in the new government was the _____ _____.

6. Nowhere in the _____ are the words "slavery" or "slaves" used.

7. _____ was the name given to those who favored the adoption of the new Constitution.

8. The _____ _____ are considered by many to be the best example of political theorizing ever produced in the United States.

9. The _____ was one of the two "lost" amendments of the twelve Bill of Rights amendments that originally went to the states in 1789.

10. President Wilson described the _____ _____ as a "constitutional convention in continuous session."

True/False   Circle the appropriate letter to indicate if the statement is true or false.

T   F   1.   The Mayflower Compact embodied the idea of majority rule as a theory of government.

T   F   2.   Thomas Paine's pamphlet, *Common Sense*, popularized the idea of the need for independence from Great Britain.

T   F   3.   According to the Declaration of Independence, these United Colonies are, and of right ought to be, free and independent states.

T   F   4.   The most fundamental weakness of the Articles of Confederation was the inability of the Congress to raise money for the militia.

T   F   5.   A majority of delegates to the Constitutional Convention were in favor of a stronger central government.

T   F   6.   The Virginia plan called for each state to have equal representation in the new government.

T   F   7.   The Anti-Federalists believed that the central government should be strengthened over the states, because the states were apt to abuse personal liberties.

T   F   8.   The delegates to the Constitutional Convention represented a good cross-section of 18th century American society.

T   F   9.   The only way to formally amend the Constitution is by a four-fifths vote of all of the state legislatures.

T   F   10. An informal way to amend the Constitution is by judicial review.

Multiple Choice. Circle the correct response.

1.   The "starving time in Virginia" refers to which colony?
     a.   Roanoke
     b.   Richmond
     c.   Jamestown
     d.   Portsmouth
     e.   Plymouth

2.   The last of the thirteen colonies to be established was
     a.   Rhode Island.
     b.   Connecticut.
     c.   New Hampshire.
     d.   New York.
     e.   Georgia.

3. The British government imposed taxes on the American colonies to pay for
    a. the war with Spain.
    b. the costs of westward expansion of colonies.
    c. the costs of the French and Indian War.
    d. the costs of exploring India.
    e. the costs of the "Tea War."

4. Thomas Paine's pamphlet, *Common Sense,*
    a. called for a cessation of hostilities against the British.
    b. pointed out in "common sense" terms why America should break with Britain.
    c. pointed out in "common sense" terms why America should not break with Britain.
    d. was a propaganda tool used by the British to gain popular consent to their governing of the colonies.
    e. apparently had very little effect on popular opinion about the revolution.

5. One of the revolutionary ideas of John Locke was the idea that people have
    a. a right to a secure job.
    b. a right to welfare if they need it.
    c. natural rights.
    d. a right to checks and balances in government.
    e. a right to vote.

6. During the Revolutionary War, the creation of state governments was strongly influenced by groups calling themselves
    a. Federalists.
    b. Democrats.
    c. Republicans.
    d. Monarchists.
    e. Royalists

7. The government under the Articles of Confederation included a
    a. president, but no congress.
    b. congress and a president.
    c. unicameral legislature.
    d. strong central government.
    e. Supreme Court.

8. Under the Articles of Confederation,
    a. each state had one vote.
    b. the national courts were the supreme authority.
    c. the congress imposed heavy taxes.
    d. the president ultimately controlled the government.
    e. a two-thirds majority was required on all laws.

9. An important accomplishment of the Articles of Confederation was
    a. the creation of a common currency.
    b. settling states' claims to western lands.
    c. the creation of national tax collections.
    d. the creation of a strong national army.
    e. the Louisiana Purchase.

10. Under the Articles of Confederation, the Congress had the power to
    a. declare war and make peace.
    b. draft soldiers into military service.
    c. compel states to pay their share of national government costs.
    d. regulate interstate and foreign commerce.
    e. collect taxes directly from the people.

11. Shay's Rebellion demonstrated that the central government
    a. had the capability to protect citizens from riots and civil unrest.
    b. could not protect the citizenry from armed rebellion.
    c. dared not confront state militias.
    d. could easily incite citizens to riot.
    e. could use the Supreme Court to resolve disputes.

12. The only state that refused to send delegates to the Constitutional Convention was
    a. New Hampshire.
    b. Rhode Island.
    c. New York.
    d. Virginia.
    e. Georgia.

13. The proceedings of the Constitutional Convention were kept secret because
    a. the delegates were doing something illegal.
    b. the public would not understand the issues involved and would create confusion.
    c. all meetings of this nature must be secret.
    d. if the proceedings were public, the delegates might have a more difficult time compromising on issues.
    e. the Monarchists were very strong in the convention.

14. The Great Compromise
    a. resulted in the Bill of Rights being added to the Constitution.
    b. broke the deadlock between the large and small states over the nature of representation in the new national government.
    c. established the Electoral College as the vehicle for electing the president.
    d. allowed George Washington to be nominated and elected the first president.
    e. created the federal court system.

15. The Madisonian Model of a government scheme refers to
    a. direct democracy.
    b. judicial review.
    c. a separation of powers.
    d. the supremacy of national laws over state laws.
    e. a plural executive.

16. The power of judicial review comes from
    a. the Constitution.
    b. the Bill of Rights.
    c. the case of *Marbury v. Madison*.
    d. executive agreements.
    e. a vote of Congress.

17. Which of the following are ways to amend the Constitution?
    a. a majority vote of citizens
    b. a majority vote of Congress
    c. a two-thirds vote of Congress
    d. judicial review by the Supreme Court
    e. the veto power of the president

18. The *Federalists Papers* were
    a. largely written by Thomas Jefferson.
    b. so brilliant, the Anti-Federalists could not respond.
    c. not very significant as political theory.
    d. responded to by Anti-Federalist political theory.
    e. written by Hamilton, Madison, and Jay.

19. The leading political figure responsible for recommending the Bill of Rights was
    a. Jefferson.
    b. Madison.
    c. Washington.
    d. Franklin.
    e. Hamilton.

20. Which of the following was NOT mentioned in the Constitution?
    a. the Electoral College
    b. the Supreme Court
    c. that national laws take priority over conflicting state laws
    d. a national convention to propose constitutional amendments
    e. that English is the national language of the United States

Short Essay   Briefly address the major concepts raised by the following questions:

1. Identify the milestone political documents that moved the colonies from the Mayflower Compact to the Constitutional Convention.

2. Trace the events and circumstances that led to the Revolutionary War.

3. Explain the compromises that evolved at the Constitutional Convention and pertained to the organization of the government.

4. Discuss both the formal and informal process of amending the Constitution.

ANSWERS TO THE PRACTICE EXAM

Fill-in-the-Blank
1. Boston Tea Party
2. natural rights
3. confederation
4. Virginia Plan
5. Great Compromise
6. Constitution
7. Federalists
8. Federalist Papers
9. 27th Amendment
10. Supreme Court

True/False

1. T	3. F	5. T	7. F	9. F
2. T	4. T	6. F	8. F	10. T

Multiple Choice

1. c	6. c	11. b	16. c
2. e	7. c	12. b	17. d
3. c	8. a	13. d	18. d
4. b	9. b	14. b	19. b
5. c	10. a	15. c	20. e

Short Essay

An adequate short answer consists of several paragraphs that relate to concepts addressed by the question. Always demonstrate your knowledge of the ideas by giving examples. The following represent major ideas that should be included in the short essay answer.

1. Identify the milestone political documents that moved the colonies from the Mayflower Compact to the Constitutional Convention.

    (Refer to the time line on page 30 to give you a good overview of the question.)
    The Mayflower Compact of 1620 was a political agreement derived from the consent of the people.
    The Fundamental Orders of Connecticut, 1639, was the first written constitution.
    The Massachusetts Body of Liberties, 1641, was the first constitution to include protection of individual rights.
    The Pennsylvania Charter of Privileges, 1701, contained a constitution and bill of rights and offered a precedent and rationale for our national Constitution.
    The Declaration of Independence, 1776, advocated independence from Great Britain.
    The Articles of Confederation, 1781, described the first attempt at an independent national government based on a confederation.

2. Trace the events and circumstances that led to the Revolutionary War.

    (Address this question in chronological/historical order.)
    Explain the reasons for British restrictions represented by the Sugar Act, Stamp Act, and Coercive Act.
    Describe the colonial response as seen in the First and Second Continental Congresses, and Paine's *Common Sense*.
    Describe and compare the Resolution of Independence and Declaration of Independence.

3. Explain the compromises that evolved at the Constitutional Convention and pertained to the organization of the government.

    Discuss the various proposed structures for the new government as seen in the Virginia Plan's proportional representation and the New Jersey Plan's equality of representation.
    Describe the Great Compromise.
    Describe the 3/5th Clause and the 1808 Ban on the Importation of Slaves
    Discuss the distribution of governmental power as represented by Madison's theories of the separation of powers and a system of checks and balances.

4. Discuss both the formal and informal process of amending the Constitution.
   - The formal process is based on two steps: proposing and ratifying amendments. (See Figure 2-3.)

   - The informal process can take place in many ways:

     o congressional legislation

     o presidential actions

     o judicial review

     o interpretation, custom, and usage

Chapter 3
FEDERALISM

CHAPTER SUMMARY

Government in the United States consists of one national government, fifty state governments, and 88,525 local governments, creating a grand total of more than 88,576. (See Table 3-1.)

Three Systems of Government

There are three basic ways of organizing governmental structures. A unitary system invests ultimate governmental authority in the national, or central, government. A confederate system is a league of independent states, each having essentially sovereign powers. A federal system divides government authority between a national government and state governments. (See Figure 3-1 for an illustration of the flow of power in the three systems.)

Why Federalism?

The United States developed a federal system because it was a practical solution that retained state traditions and local power while creating a strong national government. Federalism also solved the problems of geographical size and regional isolation. Other arguments for federalism are that it diffuses political dissatisfaction among the different governments, provides a training ground for future national leaders, allows diverse groups to develop in their own regions, and brings government closer to the people. Not every political viewpoint supported federalism. Some of the arguments against federalism are that it provides a way for powerful state and local interests to block national progress, allows for the possibility of expansion of national powers at the expense of states, and provides a way for powerful state and local interests to deny equal rights for minorities.

The Constitutional Basis for American Federalism

While the Constitution does not directly refer to federalism, it does divide governmental powers into those granted to national government, granted to state government, or prohibited to government. National government power can be described as enumerated, implied, or inherent. Enumerated powers are found in the first seventeen clauses of Article I, Section 8. Implied powers come from the necessary and proper (or "elastic") clause, the last clause of Article I, Section 8. Inherent powers come from the fact that governments have an inherent right to ensure their own survival. Powers given to state governments, called reserved powers, come from the Tenth Amendment, which states that powers not enumerated or denied are reserved to the states. A major state power is police power, which is the authority to legislate for the health, morals, safety, and welfare of the citizens of the state. National and state governments share some powers, called concurrent powers, such as the power to tax. Powers denied to government, called prohibited powers, deny powers to both national and state governments. The supremacy clause (Article VI, Paragraph 2) determines that federal laws are superior to all conflicting state and local laws.

Defining Constitutional Powers—The Early Years

To be effective over the centuries, the Constitution had to be vague and flexible. Two vague areas that were subject to the interpretation of the Supreme Court were the necessary and proper clause and the commerce clause. In the case of *McCulloch v. Maryland* (1819), Chief Justice John Marshall ruled that the necessary and proper clause of Article I, Section 8 embraces all means that are appropriate to carry out the legitimate ends of the Constitution. In *Gibbons v. Ogden* (1824), Chief Justice Marshall ruled that the power to regulate interstate commerce in Article I, Section 8 is an exclusive national power.

States' Rights and the Resort to Civil War

The Jacksonian era (1829-1837) created a climate favorable to increased states' rights, in which most southern states attempted to nullify national laws and to justify secession from the federal union. The defeat of the South in the Civil War ended the theory of secession and ultimately created a larger and more powerful national government, which for the first time imposed an income tax on its citizens. The Civil War amendments abolished slavery, defined state citizenship, and granted suffrage to African Americans.

The Continuing Dispute over the Division of Power

Although the outcome of the Civil War established the supremacy of the national government, the debate over the division of authority continued through several visions of federalism. In dual federalism, which was the prevailing model after the Civil War but faded in the 1930s, the state governments and national government were viewed as completely separate entities, like separate layers in a cake. This theory held that neither the state government nor the national government should interfere in each other's sphere as they are co-equal powers. Cooperative federalism, which was created to deal with the disaster of the Depression, advocates that state governments and the national government should cooperate in solving problems, mixing like merged layers in a marble cake. In the 1960s, another metaphor for cooperative federalism developed: picket-fence federalism. This added local government to the mix, and can be explained as though the horizontal boards in the fence represent the national, state, and local governments, while the vertical pickets represent different programs and policies in which each level of government works. Cooperative federalism was implemented largely through the administration and control of federal grants. With categorical grants, designed for specific projects of state and local governments, the national government can offload certain programs to states, which often receive the money as "free" (or requiring only nominal matching funds from the state's treasury). Before 1960, most categorical grants were formula grants; post-1960s, the government switched to offering program grants. Block grants provide federal funding for more general areas of function and are subject to fewer restrictions. Handing authority over to state governments can be hindered by federal mandates. A federal mandate is a requirement in federal legislation that forces states and local governments to comply with certain rules. (Figure 3-2 details shifts in government spending.)

The Politics of Federalism

The allocation of power between national and state governments is still a major issue that divides Americans. In its abolition of slavery, intervention in the economy, expansion of civil rights, and increased spending to combat poverty, the federal government has imposed itself into debates that some maintain fall under the rights of states. States may favor the status quo when it comes to competition among states and local economic interests. Transfer of power from the national level to the state level is called devolution and has become, since 1968, an ideological theme of the Republican party, which refers to the process as "new federalism." Under Nixon's New Federalism, categorical grants were transformed to block grants and policies of revenue sharing (unconditional financial support, later revoked) were instituted. Today, both Democrats and Republicans advocate for certain devolutions that their platforms support, so it is unclear whether the parties are separated by competing visions of federalism. Also many states believe that they can simply do a better job of providing a given service or benefit. States can tailor their programs to their specific needs and avoid the one-size-fits-all approach of the federal government.

Federalism and the Supreme Court Today

The Supreme Court has been instrumental in drawing lines between national and state powers. Since the 1990s, the Court began a general trend of giving more weight to state's rights by setting limits on federal power under the Tenth and Eleventh Amendments and the commerce clause. In *United States v. Lopez* (1995), the Court held that Congress had overreached its authority under the commerce clause when it passed the Gun-Free School Zones Act in 1990. In 1999, the Court used the Eleventh Amendment to bolster states' rights in its ruling on *Alden v. Maine*, exempting the states from lawsuits brought against them for violating federal employment law. The justices' rulings, however, have not been without contradiction. In *Nevada v. Hibbs* (2003), the Court held the state to the requirements of the federal Family and Medical Leave Act, pulling away somewhat from its previous interpretation of the Eleventh Amendment. The Tenth Amendment has also been a site of judicial exploration of the jurisdictions of the federal versus state governments, as in *Printz v. United States* (1997), which held that states couldn't be compelled to enforce or administer federal regulatory programs. More recently, the court's message on federalism has been mixed, with some rulings favoring greater states' rights and some moving towards a stronger national government. In 2007, the Court bolsters states' rights when it upheld Oregon's controversial "death with dignity" law, which allows patients with terminal illnesses to choose to end their lives early and thus alleviate suffering.

The Court then reversed course by supporting the federal government's power to seize and destroy illegal drugs over California's law legalizing the use of marijuana for medical treatment. In *Massachusetts v. EPA*, the Court expanded federal power by ruling that it was the EPA's responsibility to establish and regulate states' greenhouse gas emission standards.

KEY TERMS

block grants
categorical grants
commerce clause
concurrent powers
confederal system
cooperative federalism
devolution
dual federalism
elastic clause, or necessary and proper clause

enumerated powers
federal mandate
interstate compact
picket-fence federalism
police power
supremacy clause
unitary system

OTHER RESOURCES

A number of valuable supplements are available to students using the Schmidt, Shelley, and Bardes text. A list of suggested supplements is at the end of the chapter. Ask your instructor how to obtain these resources. One supplement is highlighted here, the Cato Institute's Web page.

E-MOCRACY EXERCISES

Direct URL: http://www.cato.org/new/pressrelease.php?id=108

Surfing Instructions:
Log on to www.cato.org
Locate the "Search" window in the upper right corner.
Type "cato news release 108" and click "search."
The article's title is "Mayor Fenty to Seek Supreme Court Review of Court Decision Striking Down D.C. Gun Ban." The search engine will list it as "Cato News Release – July 16, 2007."

Study Questions
1. How does this case illustrate our discussion of federalism?

2. In *Parker v. District of Columbia*, the D.C. Court of Appeals ruled that the individual's federal right to bear firearms trumps a state's right to ban firearms. Do you agree with the ruling?

3. Which model of federalism does this ruling support?

PRACTICE EXAM
(Answers appear at the end of this chapter.)

Fill-in-the-Blank   Supply the missing word(s) or term to complete the sentence.

1. A system of government in which power is divided between a central government and regional, or subdivisional, government is called a(n) _____ system.

2. _____ powers are those that are derived from the fact that the United States is a sovereign power among nations.

3. The Tenth Amendment establishes the _____ powers to the states.

4. The denial of power to state and national government is referred to as _____ _____.

5. The legitimate exercise of national government power _____ any action by states.

6. The issue in the *McCulloch v. Maryland* case was whether the national government has _____ powers.

7. Governors and mayors generally support _____ grants.

8. The doctrine that emphasizes a distinction between separate spheres of federal and state governmental authority is referred to as _____ _____.

9. A major set of block grants related to state _____ programs in the mid-1990s.

10. _____ _____ require state and local governments to comply with certain rules.

True/False   Circle the appropriate letter to indicate if the statement is true or false.

T   F   1. A unitary system of government is the easiest system to define.

T   F   2. The United States Constitution expressly designates that we should have a federal system of government.

T   F   3. The national government may deny the use of reserved powers to the states.

T   F   4. The Tenth Amendment provides for the reserved powers to the states.

T   F   5. Most concurrent powers of the states are specifically stated in the Constitution.

T   F   6. The Civil War permanently ended the idea that any state can claim the right to secede.

T   F   7. Chief Justice John Marshall was a strong supporter of state's rights.

T   F   8. The case of *McCulloch v. Maryland* (1819) set a precedent for a narrow interpretation of the implied powers of Congress.

T   F   9. Dual federalism emphasizes a distinction between separate federal and state spheres of sovereign authority.

T   F   10. There are great differences in prison sentences, even among counties in the same state.

Multiple choice   Circle the correct response.

1. The most popular way of ordering relations between central government and local units is by a(n)
   a. confederate system.
   b. federal system.
   c. unitary system.
   d. constitutional system.
   e. theocratic system.

2. If ultimate governmental authority rests in the hands of a central government, that is a(n)
   a. federal system.
   b. confederate system.
   c. unitary system.
   d. theocratic system.
   e. constitutional system.

3. A league of independent states, in which the central government has authority over only those matters expressly delegated to it and each state as essentially the sovereign powers, is a(n)
    a. federal system.
    b. confederate system.
    c. unitary system.
    d. democratic system.
    e. constitutional system.

4. To the framers of the Constitution, the appeal of federalism was that it
    a. allowed the states to control the process of government decision-making.
    b. retained state traditions and local powers while it established a strong national government.
    c. was acceptable to the British Parliament.
    d. did not change the status quo.
    e. provided more economic power.

5. The essential argument in *Federalist Paper No. 10* is that
    a. a unitary government is the best kind of government for a diverse society.
    b. smaller political units are likely to be dominated by a single political group.
    c. a unitary system of government is the most efficient.
    d. only with a strong chief executive can the U.S. maintain its independence in world politics.
    e. too many checks and balances will cause a weak government.

6. A special category of national powers that are NOT implied by the necessary and proper clause consists of those labeled as
    a. inherent powers.
    b. enumerated powers.
    c. extraordinary powers.
    d. elongated powers.
    e. reserved powers.

7. The constitutional concept of police powers is created by the
    a. Tenth Amendment.
    b. necessary and proper clause.
    c. interstate commerce clause.
    d. combined power clause.
    e. Supreme Court ruling in *McCulloch v. Maryland*.

8. The issue in *McCulloch v. Maryland* was
    a. judiciary supremacy of the Supreme Court.
    b. the use of delegated power by the president.
    c. the commerce clause to regulate shipping on the open seas.
    d. the use of implied powers by the national government.
    e. the use of police powers by the state.

9. Grants to state and local governments designed for very specific programs and projects are referred to as
    a. block grants.
    b. revenue sharing.
    c. unfunded mandates.
    d. picket-fence funds.
    e. categorical grants.

10. Picket-fence federalism refers to
    a. state and local governments.
    b. the restoration of more power to the national government.
    c. Congress.
    d. child labor laws.
    e. grants.

11. Because of the supremacy clause the states cannot
    a. deny citizens of another state the same privileges and immunities they extend to their own citizens.
    b. use their reserved or concurrent powers to thwart national policies.
    c. discriminate against citizens from another state.
    d. tax their citizens beyond national governmental rates.
    e. administer federal programs.

12. Picket-fence federalism added what element to the national and state governments?
    a. interest groups
    b. local governments
    c. multi-national corporations
    d. political parties
    e. special interest groups

13. In the case of *United States v. Lopez*, the Supreme Court ruled that
    a. the national government exceeded its regulatory powers.
    b. the state government exceeded its reserve powers.
    c. the local government exceeded its police powers.
    d. both state and national government exceeded constitutional powers.
    e. citizens have the right to sue government.

14. The concept of cooperative federalism was coined by political scientists during the administration of
    a. George Washington.
    b. Abraham Lincoln.
    c. Franklin D. Roosevelt.
    d. Ronald Reagan.
    e. George H. Bush.

15. The case of *United States v. Morrison* dealt with the issue of
    a. Congress overreaching its authority.
    b. states overreaching their authority.
    c. private foundations overreaching their authority.
    d. multi-national corporations overreaching their authority.
    e. the Justice Department overreaching its authority.

16. Block grants are tools that help establish
    a. less restrictions on state and local governments.
    b. dual federalism.
    c. more strings on state and local governments.
    d. no difference in federalism.
    e. a more active welfare state.

17. Federal mandates are
    a. programs funded by Congress.
    b. programs funded by states.
    c. programs required by the national government but not necessarily fully funded.
    d. being phased out by Congress.
    e. programs funded by local government.

18. Which Supreme Court case involved an issue of the Eleventh Amendment?
    a. *McCulloch v. Maryland*
    b. *U.S. v. Lopez*
    c. *U.S. v. Morrison*
    d. *Alden v. Maine*
    e. *Printz v. United States*

19. The Gun Free School Zones Act was ruled
    a. constitutional in *Kimel v. Florida.*
    b. constitutional in *Alden v. Maine.*
    c. unconstitutional in *U.S. v. Morrison.*
    d. unconstitutional in *Printz v. U.S.*
    e. unconstitutional in *U.S. v. Lopez.*

20. Devolution refers to
    a. the transfer of power from a national or central government to a state or local government.
    b. the evolution of the races.
    c. the teaching of evolution and intelligent design.
    d. the disillusionment of the voting public.
    e. none of the above.

Short Essay Questions   Briefly address the major concepts raised by the following questions.

1. Discuss the three ways of organizing relations between a central government and local governmental units.

2. Identify and explain the division of powers between the national and state governments in the Constitution.

3. Trace and explain the debate over the division of powers between national and state government, since the Civil War.

4. Discuss the latest trends in our federal system, including federal mandates, Supreme Court decisions, and competitive federalism.

ANSWERS TO THE PRACTICE EXAM

Fill-in-the-Blank
1. federal
2. Inherent
3. police
4. prohibited powers
5. preempts
6. implied
7. block
8. dual federalism
9. welfare
10. Federal mandates

True/False

1. T	3. F	5. F	7. F	9. T
2. F	4. T	6. T	8. F	10. T

Multiple Choice

1. c	6. a	11. b	16. a
2. c	7. a	12. b	17. c
3. b	8. d	13. a	18. d
4. b	9. e	14. c	19. c
5. b	10. a	15. a	20. a

Short Essay

An adequate short answer consists of several paragraphs that relate to concepts addressed by the question. Always demonstrate your knowledge of the ideas by giving examples. The following represent major ideas that should be included in the short essay answer.

1. Discuss the three ways of organizing relations between a central government and local governmental units.

(Refer to Figure 3-1 for a view of the three ways and how power flows in each.)
Unitary system—a centralized governmental system in which ultimate governmental authority rests in the hands of the national, or central, government.
Confederal system—a system consisting of a league of independent states, each having essentially sovereign powers.
Federal system—a system in which power is divided between a central government and regional, or sub-divisional, governments.

2. Identify and explain the division of powers between the national and state governments in the Constitution.

Expressed or enumerated powers are specific national government powers from Article 1, Section 8.
Implied powers are national government powers from the necessary and proper clause.
Concurrent powers are powers shared jointly by national and state governments.
Reserved powers are state powers from the Tenth Amendment to the Constitution.
The supremacy clause makes federal law supreme over all conflicting state and local laws.

3.. Trace and explain the debate over the division of powers between national and state government since the Civil War.

Dual federalism is the system of government in which the individual states and the national government each retain sovereign supremacy within their own spheres of operation.
Cooperative federalism is the system in which the states and national government should cooperate in solving problems. Federal grants are the main factor in developing cooperative federalism.
Picket-fence federalism adds local governments to the state and federal mix when analyzing overlapping involvement in programs.

4.. Discuss the latest trends in our federal system, including federal mandates, Supreme Court decisions, and competitive federalism.

- Federal mandates are requirements that force states and local government to comply with certain rules, and are a major barrier to new federalism. These mandates are not necessarily funded by the national government.
- *Printz v. U.S.* struck down the provision of the Brady Bill that required state employees to check the background of prospective handgun purchasers.

- *U.S. v. Lopez* held that the Gun-Free School Zones Act of 1990 exceeded the authority of Congress under the commerce clause of the Constitution.
- The Supreme Court ruled that Congress had overstepped its authority under the commerce clause and Tenth and Eleventh Amendments in the cases of *United States v. Morrison*, *Alden v. Maine*, and *Kimel v. Florida Board of Regents*.

Chapter 4
CIVIL LIBERTIES

CHAPTER SUMMARY

Civil liberties are individual rights that are protected from government action and interference, as outlined in the Bill of Rights. Over the years, interpretation of the Bill of Rights has allowed conflicts over and changes in the freedoms that citizens enjoy under the U.S. government.

The Bill of Rights

Most citizens are not aware that the Bill of Rights originally applied only to the national government. The Fourteenth Amendment, ratified in 1868, seemed to apply civil liberties guaranteed by the national constitution to the states. Incorporation theory holds that the protections of the Bill of Rights are applied to state governments by the Fourteenth Amendment's due process clause. The Supreme Court has gradually— and not completely—accepted this theory. The first right to be incorporated was freedom of speech, in *Gitlow v. New York* (1925). (See Table 4-1 for a list of cases incorporating various aspects of the Bill of Rights.)

Freedom of Religion

The First Amendment to the Constitution begins with two basic principles of freedom of religion: the establishment clause and the free exercise clause. The First Amendment begins with the words "Congress shall make no law respecting an establishment of religion." The establishment clause, which put up, in Thomas Jefferson's words, a "wall of separation of Church and State," covers such conflicts as state and local aid to religion, school prayer, and the teaching of evolution versus creationism. In *Lemon v. Kurtzman* (1971), the Supreme Court ruled that direct state aid could not be used to subsidize religious instruction. This case created a three-part "Lemon test" for the establishment clause. In *Agostini v. Felton* (1997), the Court reversed itself, ruling that the use of federal funds for disadvantaged students attending religious schools did not violate the establishment clause. The use of public fund school vouchers for religious education has so far been upheld by the Supreme Court, but important issues remain. In *Engel v. Vitale* (1962), the Court ruled that school-sponsored prayer was in violation of the establishment clause. The *Wallace v. Jaffree* (1985) ruling struck down a minute of silent prayer in Alabama. Prayer outside the classroom was also limited in *Lee v. Weisman* (1992), which addressed graduation ceremonies. The issue of teaching intelligent design was decided in *Edwards v. Aguillard* (1987), which ruled that teaching the Judeo-Christian story of creation in a publicly funded, secular biology course was unconstitutional. In recent years, the Supreme Court seemed to be lowering the barrier between church and state. In 1995, in *Rosenberger v. University of Virginia*, the Court ruled that the University must fund a Christian newsletter, if it is funding other campus groups' newsletters. The free exercise clause has usually focused on striking a balance between religious belief and religious practice. Religious practices can be regulated, as in the case of *Oregon v. Smith* (1990), in which two Native American drug counselors were fired for using peyote, an illegal drug, in their religious services. In 1997, the *Boerne v. Flores* case ruled the Religious Freedom Restoration Act (RFRA) of 1993 as unconstitutional for granting religious authorities too much power. Today, the No Child Left Behind Act ensures that schools will not overly restrict religion by withholding funds from schools that abide too strictly by the overturning of RFRA.

Freedom of Expression

Freedom of expression is probably the most often used right that Americans have, but this right cannot be used to say anything at any time and/or any place. Prior restraint to regulate speech, which is censorship, has usually been ruled unconstitutional by the Court. In one of the most famous cases, *New York Times v. U.S.* (1971), the Pentagon Papers case, the Supreme Court ruled that *The New York Times* had the right to publish the information about the Vietnam War. The Court has also given protection to symbolic speech, involving nonverbal expressions such as those in opposition to the government. In a highly controversial case, *Texas v. Johnson* (1989), flag burning was given protection as symbolic speech; a 2003 ruling did not, however, afford the same protection to the burning of a cross as a symbol of racist terror. The advertising statements of commercial speech are protected as well, though factual inaccuracies within that speech are not. The Supreme Court has established some reasonable restrictions on free speech, and entire areas of speech are not considered constitutionally protected. The clear and present danger test used by Justice Oliver Wendell Holmes in a case in 1919 restricted speech that could provoke a "clear and present danger" to public order. The bad-tendency rule from *Gitlow v. N.Y.* (1925) limited speech that might lead to some "evil." The "grave and probable danger rule" of 1951 modified Holmes' rule to justify invasion of free speech. But the *Brandenburg v. Ohio* (1969) ruling, with its "incitement test," again broadened the protection given to advocacy speech. Obscenity, slander, child and "virtual" pornography, campus speech, and hate speech have not been protected by the Court. There are difficulties defining obscenity, but in *Miller v. California* (1973) the Court created a four-part list of requirements for determining obscenity that have been applied widely and inconsistently. Pornography involving minors is not protected, but its connection to the Internet is making this issue very complicated. Slander is not protected, as individuals are protected from defamation of character. The debate around campus speech is the issue of whether or not the funds of one student's tuition should be used, in effect, to subsidize organizations to which that student objects.

Freedom of the Press

The actions of the press can be viewed as printed speech, which means that many concepts of freedom of expression apply to the written word. Libel, the written defamation of a person's character, is a major concern of mass media today. The Supreme Court in *New York Times v. Sullivan* (1964) gave some protection to media by ruling that public figures who sue for libel must prove actual malice on the part of the media. This greater burden of proof for public figures allows for the criticism of public employees and discussions of differences of opinion without fear of lawsuits. Another important issue for a free press is the conflict between the public's right to know and the rights of individuals or the police in the criminal justice system. In *Gannett Company v. De Pasquale* (1979), the Supreme Court ruled that a judge could issue a gag order to protect a defendant's right to a fair trial, shielded from excessive news publicity. Broadcast media generally have more restrictions than print: the movie industry has its own ratings board to regulate its output, and radio and television fall under the control of the Federal Communications Commission.

The Right to Assemble and to Petition the Government

This right often involves speech and press issues, since few demonstrations involve silent protests. The key issue is how to balance this right with the necessity for public officials to control traffic and maintain public order. In 1977, the Supreme Court upheld the First Amendment rights of Nazis who had been denied the permits, and thus the freedom, to march by the city of Skokie, Illinois. Other issues include the assembly (or possibly "loitering") of street gangs and the right of citizens to assemble online.

More Liberties under Scrutiny: Matters of Privacy

The right to privacy has no explicit mention in the Constitution. It stems from the Supreme Court case *Griswold v. Connecticut* (1965). The Court ruled that the right to privacy stems from "penumbras" in the First, Third, Fourth, Fifth, and Ninth Amendments in the Bill of Rights. The first major application of privacy rights was *Roe v. Wade* (1973), in which the Supreme Court accepted the argument that laws against abortion violate a woman's right to privacy. This decision has created probably the most divisive public policy issue in America, even though later Court decisions have placed restrictions on abortion rights. A second major application of the right to privacy is the right to die. The New Jersey Supreme Court in the Quinlan case in 1976 established this principle. The U.S. Supreme Court modified this concept in *Cruzan v. Director, Missouri Department of Health* (1990). The Cruzan case has lead to the creation of "living wills" and other documents to provide safeguards to the right to die. In a related issue, the Court has left the ruling on the right to assisted suicide to state governments; only Oregon allows it. A major privacy rights issue today revolves around security situations, an emphasis produced by the attacks of September 11, 2001, and encompassing the USA Patriot Act and "roving" warrantless wiretaps. In both *Doe v. Ashcroft* and *Doe v. Gonzales* the Court ruled that certain portions of the Patriot Act were unconstitutional.

The Great Balancing Act: The Rights of the Accused versus the Rights of Society

One of the Constitution's most difficult areas of balance between the rights of individuals and the rights of society involves the rights of those accused of criminal offenses. The Fourth, Fifth, Sixth, and Eighth Amendments deal with the rights of criminal defendants. (See a complete listing of these rights in the book.)

During the 1960s, the Supreme Court greatly expanded the rights of accused persons. In 1963, *Gideon v. Wainwright* granted a poor defendant the right to an attorney. In 1966, *Miranda v. Arizona* required police to inform an individual of his or her constitutional rights prior to questioning. Recent Court decisions have placed some restrictions on the Miranda ruling, in a continuing effort to find the right balance between individual and societal rights. The exclusionary rule, a judicial policy which prohibits the admission of illegally obtained evidence during a trial, was applied to federal courts in 1914. The concept was first applied to state courts in the case of *Mapp v. Ohio* (1961). (Refer back to Table 4-1 for incorporation cases.) Again, recent Court decisions have provided some exceptions for police officers who act in "good faith."

The Death Penalty

The death penalty is one of the most debated aspects of our criminal justice system because of the Eighth Amendment protection against "cruel and unusual" punishment. In 1972, the Supreme Court ruled in *Furman v. Georgia* that the death penalty was random and arbitrary. This case was based on the existing state laws on the death penalty, which were changed post-ruling to be more precise and then adopted by many states. (See Figure 4-1.) In 1996, Congress passed the Anti-Terrorism and Effective Death Penalty Act. This sharply reduced the time for death row appeals, from an average of ten to twelve years to six to eight years. Despite this 1996 Act, death sentence rates are falling due to increased public awareness of wrongful convictions and botched lethal injections that some consider "cruel and unusual" punishment. In the 2002 case *Ring v. Arizona*, the Court determined that only juries, not judges, could pass down a death penalty verdict. It is believed that this ruling has also contributed to the decline in death penalty sentences.

KEY TERMS

actual malice
arraignment
clear and present danger test
commercial speech
defamation of character
establishment clause
exclusionary rule
free exercise clause

gag order
incorporation theory
libel
prior restraint
public figure
slander
symbolic speech
writ of *habeas corpus*

OTHER RESOURCES

A number of valuable supplements are available to students using the Schmidt, Shelley, and Bardes text. A list of suggested supplements is at the end of the chapter. Ask your instructor how to obtain these resources. One supplement is highlighted here, flag protection.

E-MOCRACY EXERCISES

Direct URL: www.freedomforum.org/packages/first/Flag/timeline.htm

Surfing Instructions:
Log on to www.freedomforum.org/packages/first/Flag/timeline.htm
Read through the historical timeline.
At the top of the page, select "Editorials."
Select and read one or two of the editorials listed.

Study Questions
1.   Is the article's author in favor of, or against, the ratification of an anti-flag-burning amendment?
2.   What is the fundamental premise for the author's argument for or against?
3.   What is your belief on the need for a constitutional amendment regarding this issue?

PRACTICE EXAM
(Answers appear at the end of this chapter.)

Fill-in-the-Blank   Supply the missing word(s) or term to complete the sentence.

1. _____ _____ involves restraining the government's actions against individuals.

2. It was not until the _____ Amendment was ratified that our Constitution explicitly guaranteed due process of law to everyone.

3. The Lemon test explains the concept of the _____ _____ in freedom of religion.

4. According to the _____ _____ rule, speech or other First Amendment freedoms may be curtailed if there is a possibility that such expression might lead to some evil.

5. The burning of the American flag as part of a peaceful protest is expressive conduct considered _____ _____ .

6. For slander to be judged as defamation of character there must be a _____ _____ witness.

7. Only when a statement is made with_____ _____ can a public official receive damages for libel.

8. In the 1990s, the most controversial aspect of the right-to-die was _____ assisted suicide.

9. The _____, _____, _____, and _____ Amendments specifically deal with the rights of criminal defendants.

10. The use of illegally seized evidence is prohibited in a trial because of the _____ rule.

True/False   Circle the appropriate letter to indicate if the statement is true or false.

T   F   1. The concept of civil liberties mainly refers to laws passed by Congress to limit government power.

T   F   2. As originally presented, the Bill of Rights limited only the powers of the states, not the national government.

T   F   3. Most of the guarantees in the Bill of Rights now apply to the fifty states.

T   F   4. The use of state aid to private religious schools has generally been accepted by the Supreme Court.

T   F   5. For the most part, Americans are very limited in their ability to criticize public officials.

T   F   6. The federal courts have not extended constitutional protections of free speech to matter that is considered obscene.

T   F   7. Gag orders restrict the publication of news about a trial in progress or a pretrial hearing.

T   F   8. The right of privacy is explicitly guaranteed in the Bill of Rights.

T   F   9. The Webster and Planned Parenthood decisions have made it much easier to obtain a legal abortion.

T   F   10. The United States has one of the highest violent crime rates in the world.

Multiple Choice   Circle the correct response.

1. When we are speaking of civil liberties, we are referring to limitations on government as outlined in the
    a. Declaration of Independence.
    b. Magna Carta.
    c. Articles of Confederation.
    d. Second Amendment.
    e. Bill of Rights.

2. The view that most of the protections of the Bill of Rights are included under the Fourteenth Amendment's protection against state government is called the
    a. inclusionary theory.
    b. nullification theory.
    c. necessary and proper theory.
    d. incorporation theory.
    e. symbolic speech theory.

3. The three-part Lemon Test concerns the issue of
    a. symbolic speech.
    b. state aid to church-related schools.
    c. presentation of evidence before a grand jury.
    d. the right to die.
    e. incorporation.

4. The free exercise clause in the First Amendment does not prevent the government from curtailing religious practices that

    a. work against public policy and the public welfare.
    b. infringe on citizen's sensitivities.
    c. are defined by media as "cult" religions.
    d. are a willful violation of the Pledge of Allegiance at public schools.
    e. are door-to-door solicitations.

5. According to the "clear and present danger" test,
    a. a speech must be unclear as to its intent for it to be ruled unconstitutional.
    b. the action called for must be constitutionally "vague" in order to be ruled unconstitutional.
    c. free speech can be curbed if such speech would cause a condition that Congress has the power to prevent.
    d. free speech may not be curbed, because speech alone cannot bring about action.
    e. only symbolic speech can bring about danger.

6. The burning of an American flag in a peaceful protest is an example of
    a. a violation of the Constitution.
    b. a violation of the bad tendency doctrine.
    c. a protected action under the clear and present danger concept.
    d. a protected action under the symbolic speech concept.
    e. an issue not yet decided by the Supreme Court.

7. Paid advertising can be constitutionally protected as a form of
    a. commercial speech.
    b. symbolic speech.
    c. exempted speech.
    d. private speech.
    e. vague speech.

8. The *Miller v. California* case created a list of requirements that apply to
    a. abortion.
    b. religious freedom.
    c. obscenity.
    d. libel.
    e. the right to remain silent.

9. Child pornography has been ruled by the Supreme Court to be
    a. a constitutionally protected form of speech.
    b. an unconstitutionally protected form of speech which can be regulated by the state.
    c. a constitutionally protected form of speech only in the privacy of your home.
    d. a constitutionally protected form of speech only on the Internet.
    e. in a vague area that the federal courts have not ruled on.

10. Public officials may sue for libel if they can prove the statement
    a. was false.
    b. hurt the official's reputation.
    c. hurt the official's feelings.
    d. was made with actual malice.
    e. was made during an election campaign.

11. Gag orders are
    a. designed to eliminate illegal speech.
    b. designed to eliminate unlawful assembly.
    c. restrictions on the publication of news concerning pretrial hearing or trials in progress.
    d. part of the controversy over the death penalty.
    e. ruled unconstitutional in *Gannett Co. v. De Pasquale*.

12. The *Roe v. Wade* case decided the abortion issue on the basis of
    a. freedom of religion.
    b. freedom of speech.
    c. the right to privacy.
    d. the incorporation concept.
    e. the right to assemble and petition the government.

13. The exclusionary rule prohibits
    a. defendants from testifying in their own behalf.
    b. improperly obtained evidence from being used by prosecutors.
    c. a spouse from testifying in a criminal case.
    d. the defense counsel from having access to the prosecution's evidence.
    e. television cameras in the courtroom.

14. The exclusionary rule was first extended to state court proceedings in the Supreme Court case of
    a. *Nix v. Williams*.
    b. *Miranda v. Arizona*.
    c. *Mapp v. Ohio*.
    d. *Betts v. Brady*.
    e. *Gregg v. Georgia*.

15. A technically incorrect search warrant can be legal under the concept of
    a. the Miranda rule.
    b. the "good faith" exception.
    c. the unreasonable search and seizure.
    d. the right to an attorney if you cannot afford one.
    e. the right to an appeal in a felony case.

16. The case that ruled against the right to commit suicide was
    a. *Cruzan v. Director, Missouri Dept. of Health.*
    b. *Furman v. Georgia.*
    c. *Washington v. Glucksberg.*
    d. *Miranda v. Arizona.*
    e. *Gregg v. Georgia.*

17. The Anti-Terrorism and Effective Death Penalty Act provided for
    a. immediate execution after the guilty verdict.
    b. execution within a month after the guilty verdict.
    c. a severe time limit on death-row appeals.
    d. the so-called "three strikes and you're out" procedure.
    e. mandatory DNA testing before execution.

18. According to the text, a growing concern about free speech on the Internet is
    a. slander.
    b. obscenity.
    c. hate speech.
    d. fraud in commercial speech.
    e. symbolic speech.

19. In the case of *Board of Regents of the University of Wisconsin System v. Southworth* (2000), the Court ruled that the use of student activity fees to fund extracurricular groups whose causes some students found offensive was
    a. not covered by the U.S. Constitution.
    b. constitutional.
    c. constitutional with equal time for both sides.
    d. unconstitutional because of the First Amendment.
    e. unconstitutional because of the Fifth Amendment.

20. The Supreme Court, in the 2007 *Gonzales* cases, ruled that "partial-birth" abortions are
    a. unconstitutional.
    b. not covered by *Roe v. Wade*.
    c. constitutional.
    d. constitutional, only if passed by state legislatures.
    e. constitutional, only if passed by Congress.

Short Essay Questions   Briefly address the major concepts raised by the following questions:

1. Explain the historical context for the importance of the Bill of Rights within the Constitution.

2. Identify and explain the two concepts of freedom of religion contained in the First Amendment.

3. Discuss the important principles established by the Supreme Court regarding freedom of speech and press.

4. Outline and discuss the rights of an individual accused of a crime.

ANSWERS TO THE PRACTICE EXAM

Fill-in-the-Blank
1. Civil liberties
2. Fourteenth
3. establishment clause

4. bad tendency
5. symbolic speech
6. third party
7. actual malice
8. physician
9. Fourth, Fifth, Sixth, Eighth
10. exclusionary

True/False

| 1. F | 3. T | 5. F | 7. T | 9. F |
| 2. F | 4. F | 6. T | 8. F | 10. T |

Multiple Choice

1. e	6. d	11. c	16. c
2. d	7. a	12. c	17. c
3. b	8. c	13. b	18. c
4. a	9. b	14. c	19. d
5. c	10. d	15. b	20. c

Short Essay

An adequate short answer consists of several paragraphs that relate to concepts addressed by the question. Always demonstrate your knowledge of the ideas by giving examples. The following represent major ideas that should be included in the short essay answer.

1. Explain the historical context of the importance of the Bill of Rights within the Constitution.

Few specific restrictions on government were contained in the Constitution.
The Bill of Rights did not apply to state governments.
The Fourteenth Amendment guaranteed civil liberties of the Constitution that applied to the states, which is called incorporation.
Only gradually, on a case-by-case basis—but never completely—has the Supreme Court accepted incorporation.
Once a right has been incorporated, states are required to protect that specific civil liberty.
(See Table 4-1 for a list of cases incorporating different constitutional rights.)

2. Identify and explain the two concepts of freedom of religion contained in the First Amendment.

The establishment clause prohibits official government support of religion.
Lemon v. Kurtzman (1971) creates a three-part test of this concept.
   • *Engle v. Vitale* (1962) ruled that official prayer in public school is unconstitutional.
   • The teaching of evolution cannot be banned, and the Judeo-Christian story of creation cannot be taught.
The free exercise of religion shall not be prohibited.
Religious beliefs are absolute while religious practices, which can work against public policy and public welfare, may be restricted.
Oregon v. Smith (1990) ruled that Native Americans could be denied unemployment benefits when fired from a state job for using peyote in their religious services.
Congress passed the Religious Freedom Restoration Act (RFRA) in 1993 to require all levels of government to "accommodate religious conduct."
City of Boerne v. Flores (1997) ruled the RFRA law unconstitutional.

3.   Discuss the important principles established by the Supreme Court for freedom of speech and press.
Freedom of speech has never been considered absolute, so some restrictions are permitted.
Oliver Wendell Holmes ruled in 1919 that speech that provokes a "clear and present danger" is not
constitutionally protected and can be restricted by Congress.
- *Gitlow v. New York* (1925) held that any expression that might lead to some "evil" is not protected.
- However, in *The New York Times v. U.S.* (1971), the Court ruled that prior restraint or censorship is unconstitutional.

Symbolic speech and commercial speech have received constitutional protection.
- *Texas v. Johnson* (1989) ruled that the burning of an American flag in a peaceful protest is protected as symbolic speech.

Some speech has never been constitutionally protected.
- *Miller v. California* (1973) established a formal list of requirements for obscenity, which are not protected.
- Slander, the public uttering of a false statement that harms a person's reputation, is not protected.
- Hate speech and child pornography can be regulated in some cases.

Freedom of the press can be viewed as printed speech, so many of the same concepts apply.
- Libel is the written defamation of a person's reputation, but the press has some limited protection from libel.
- *The New York Times v. Sullivan* (1964) created the ruling that a public figure must prove actual malice on the part of media to be able to sue for libel.
- Another significant free press issue involves conflict between free press and a criminal suspect's right to a fair trial. *Gannett Company v. De Pasquale* (1979) provided for judges to issue gag orders to restrict the publication of news about pretrial hearings or trials in progress.
- Broadcast media have generally not been protected in ways similar to published materials. The FCC regulates radio and television, and the film industry regulates itself.

4. Outline and discuss the right of an individual accused of a crime.
In the Bill of Rights, the Fourth, Fifth, Sixth, and Eighth Amendments deal with rights of criminal defendants.
The process is divided into three parts:
1.   Limits on the conduct of police officers and prosecutors
2.   A defendant's pretrial rights
3.   Trial rights

The Fourth Amendment protects against an unreasonable search and seizure of evidence. The exclusionary rule prevents this evidence from being admitted at trial. *Mapp v. Ohio* extended the exclusionary rule to state courts.
The Fifth Amendment provides for the right to remain silent, to be informed of the charges, and the right to legal counsel. *Miranda v. Arizona* dealt with the right to be informed of your rights.
The Sixth Amendment provides for legal counsel during a trial, even if the defendant cannot afford one. *Gideon v. Wainwright* applied this to felony offenses.
- The Eighth Amendment prohibits excessive bail or fines, as well as cruel and unusual punishment.

Chapter 5
CIVIL RIGHTS

CHAPTER SUMMARY

The term "civil rights" refers to the rights of all Americans to equal treatment under law. The history of civil rights in America is the struggle of various groups to be free from discriminatory treatment.

African Americans and the Consequences of Slavery in the United States

Before 1863, the Constitution protected slavery. In *Dred Scott v. Sanford* (1857), the Supreme Court provided its support for the institution of slavery and ruled that slaves were neither citizens nor entitled to the rights and privileges of citizenship. President Lincoln's Emancipation Proclamation in 1863 and the passage of the Thirteenth, Fourteenth, and Fifteenth Amendments to the Constitution ended constitutional support for inequality. The Thirteenth Amendment prohibited slavery. The Fourteenth Amendment stated, among other things, that no state could deny any person equal protection of the laws. The Fifteenth Amendment stated that the right to vote could not be abridged because of race. Although these are considered routine protections today, at the time these ideas were revolutionary. From 1865 to 1875, the Republican-controlled Congress passed several civil rights acts. The Supreme Court ruled these acts unconstitutional, concluding that the Constitution prohibited only state discrimination, not the discriminatory acts of individuals. One of the most significant of the Court's decisions was *Plessy v. Ferguson* (1896), in which the doctrine of "separate but equal" was given constitutional approval under the Fourteenth Amendment's equal protection clause. "Separate but equal" was an oxymoronic device in which states would require separate facilities and opportunities for the different races while maintaining the façade of equality. The states also found ways to prevent African Americans from exercising their newly-granted right to vote. When federal troops that occupied the South were withdrawn in 1877, these states imposed any number of devices intended to restrict the right to vote, including the grandfather clause, poll taxes, and literacy tests. The white primary was finally ruled unconstitutional in the 1944 case of *Smith v. Allwright*. The end of the separate but equal doctrine began in the 1930s with a series of lawsuits designed to admit African Americans to graduate and professional schools. These lawsuits culminated in the unanimous Supreme Court decision in *Brown v. Board of Education of Topeka* in 1954, which determined that public school segregation violates the equal protection clause of the Fourteenth Amendment. The Court concluded that separate is inherently unequal and ended de jure segregation. De facto segregation, however, had to be battled with methods like court-ordered busing of students across neighborhoods. Recently, the focus on schools has shifted from desegregation to the goal of providing better education across the board, regardless of the racial makeup of a school. Spearheaded by the 2001 No Child Left Behind Act, this initiative's goal was to close the test-score gaps between white and minority students by 2014. Prior to its 2007 reauthorization, a number of studies have illustrated that little or no change has occurred.

The Civil Rights Movement

The *Brown* decision was a moral victory, but it did little to change the underlying structure of segregation outside of public schools. In 1955, an African American woman named Rosa Parks refused to give up her seat on a bus to a white man. She was arrested and fined. Thus began the civil rights protests that would eventually end racial segregation. Martin Luther King, Jr., a Baptist minister, organized a year-long boycott of the Montgomery, Alabama bus line, the success of which propelled King to national leadership of the civil rights movement. The culmination of the movement came in 1963, when Dr. King, with the intent to spark support for civil rights legislation, led a march on Washington D.C. and gave his famous "I have a dream" speech. His tactics of nonviolence and civil disobedience were not the only approaches, however; the black power movement, espoused by Malcolm X and others, took a more militant view of the conflict.

The Climax of the Civil Rights Movement

In passing the Civil Rights Act of 1964, Congress created the most far-reaching bill on civil rights in modern times. This legislation targeted discrimination in the areas of public accommodations such as hotels and restaurants. It was followed the next year by the Voting Rights Act of 1965, which eliminated discriminatory voter registration laws and authorized federal officials to register voters, primarily in the south. Subsequent amendments to the Voting Rights Act granted protections, such as bilingual ballots, to other minorities. The Civil Rights Act of 1968 banned discrimination in housing and subsequent legislation provided protections for mortgage-loan applicants. Today, although there is increased voter participation among all minorities, there are still lingering social and economic disparities that are often not perceived by white Americans. Despite these disparities, members of minority groups are achieving the highest positions in our nation as illustrated by the following: Former National Security Advisor and current Secretary of State, Dr. Condoleezza Rice; Former Chairman of the Joint Chiefs of Staff, General Colin Powell; Senator Barack Obama's (D/IL.) 2007 bid for the presidency.

Women's Struggle for Equal Rights

Women first became involved politically in the movement to abolish slavery. Spurred by this effort, Lucretia Mott and Elizabeth Cady Stanton organized the first women's rights convention in 1848. The 1870 campaign to ratify the Fifteenth Amendment, giving voting rights to African American men, split the women's suffrage movement. However, women successfully campaigned for passage of the Nineteenth Amendment, which enfranchised women and was ratified in 1920. (See Table 5-1 for the year that women gained the right to vote in other countries.) After achieving the right to vote, women engaged in little political activity until the 1960s, when the feminist movement called for political, economic, and social equality for women. The feminist movement attempted to obtain the ratification of an Equal Rights Amendment to the Constitution in the 1970s, but the necessary 38 states failed to ratify. After this defeat, the women's movement turned its attention to other issues, including domestic violence, abortion, pornography, gender discrimination, and increasing the number of women in government. Although to date no major political party has nominated a woman for president, women have run for the vice-presidency and serve as members of the cabinet and the Supreme Court. In 2007, Hillary Clinton became the first woman to run directly for the presidency. In 2002, Nancy Pelosi of California became the leader of the Democratic Party in the United States House of Representatives and, after the Democratic victories of 2006, served as the first female Speaker of the House. In 2008, the House of Representatives contained 71 women and the Senate 16.

Gender-Based Discrimination in the Workplace

Title VII of the Civil Rights Act of 1964 prohibited gender discrimination in employment, including sexual harassment. Supreme Court cases such as *Faragher v. City of Boca Raton* (1998) and *Burlington Industries v. Ellerth* (1998) established that employers were liable for sexual harassment if they did not exercise reasonable care to prevent and promptly correct any sexually harassing behavior. In another 1998 case, *Oncale v. Sundowner Offshore Services, Inc.,* the Supreme Court ruled that Title VII protection should be extended to cover situations in which individuals are harassed by members of the same gender. Another important issue for women in the workplace has been wage discrimination. Although the Equal Pay Act of 1963 was designed to provide for equal wages, a woman still earns less than a man performing the same job, even with increasing wage parity. As of 2007, a college educated woman earns 74.7 cents for every dollar earned by a college educated man. This figure is potentially a plateau as it is nearly identical to the 75.7 cents identified a decade ago. Some of the suggested reasons for the pay differential are that jobs traditionally held by women, such as child care or clerical positions, are lower-paying positions and that corporate "glass ceilings" can prevent women from reaching the highest-paid, executive positions in businesses.

Immigration, Latinos, and Civil Rights

Today immigration rates are the highest they have been since their peak in the early twentieth century. Since 1977, more than eighty percent of immigrants have come from Latin America or Asia. Another issue of consideration is the nation's fertility rate. The average woman has 2.1 children which leads to a stable population replacement. Latino's, however, have an average replacement of 2.9 which, when combined with immigration, suggest a strong long-term increase in the U.S.' Latino population. In recent years the nation has become focused on the question of illegal immigration and what should be done about it. The majority of people entering the United States illegally come from Mexico in search of work. In addition to the argument that they are taking jobs from American citizens, another controversial aspect of their presence involves the demands that illegal immigrants and their families place on social and medical services. As illustrated by the failed attempts of the 110th Congress' at immigration reform in 2007, lawmakers are dramatically split over the issue of how to treat those who are in the country illegally. Some lawmakers are calling for amnesty, others creating a schedule by which they could become citizens, and still others are demanding that they be returned to their home countries. Both legal and illegal immigrants have a degree of constitutional protection. Before deportation of an illegal immigrant can occur, they must receive a deportation hearing under the 14th Amendment's due process clause. If, however, the immigrant—legal or illegal—is declared to be a terrorist, the Supreme Court has affirmed that they can be deported immediately without a hearing. Another issue concerns the education of those who are in this country with few or no English skills. Both Congress and the Supreme Court have, in the past, supported the rights of those who require bilingual education. In recent years, however, resentment and resistance has grown over the issue of bilingual education, as demonstrated by California's passing a ballot initiative that ends bilingual education in the state.

Affirmative Action

Affirmative action refers to any policy designed to give special consideration to traditionally disadvantaged groups in an effort to overcome the present effects of past discrimination. Such policy was challenged in the 1978 case of *University of California v. Bakke,* which involved admission policies at UC-Davis Medical School. Alan Bakke argued that the affirmative action plan that used a racial quota acted as reverse discrimination against those who do not have minority status. The Supreme Court agreed, though its decision was complex. While the divided Court stated that quotas were unacceptable in making admissions decisions, it also stated that race could be considered, along with many other factors, in shaping a student body that would possess the attribute of diversity. A lower federal court expressed its disagreement with the Supreme Court in *Hopwood v. Texas* (1996), ruling that any use of race in making admissions decisions violated the Fourteenth Amendment. In 2003, however, the Supreme Court upheld the admission policy of the University of Michigan law school, supporting the school's practice of considering race as part of a complete examination of an applicant's background. In the 2007 case, *Parents Involved in Community Schools v. Seattle School District*, the Court declared that both Louisville, Kentucky's and Seattle, Washington's attempts to integrate public schools via their admissions guidelines was unconstitutional.

Special Protection for Older Americans

Age discrimination is potentially the most widespread form of discrimination because it can affect everyone at some point in life. Congress passed the Age Discrimination Employment Act in 1967, which protects workers over the age of 40. An amendment to the law passed in 1978 prohibited mandatory retirement of most workers under the age of 70, and in 1986 mandatory retirement rules were struck down entirely for all but a select few occupations (such as firefighting).

Securing Rights for Persons with Disabilities

Landmark legislation to protect the rights of persons with disabilities was achieved with the passage of the Americans with Disabilities Act of 1990 (ADA). This law requires employers to "reasonably accommodate" the needs of persons with disabilities. While many applaud the objective of allowing those with disabilities to reach their full potential, critics focus on the costs of complying with, and the difficulty of interpreting, the ADA. From 1999 on, the Supreme Court has issued several rulings that have put limits on the ADA. Protections for correctable afflictions (including severe nearsightedness, bipolar disorder, and diabetes) were removed in the *Sutton v. United Airlines, Inc.* (1999) case, and a 2001 ruling determined that states cannot be sued under the federal ADA. In the 2002 case, *Toyota Manufacturing, Kentucky, Inc. v. Williams,* the Court further limited the ADA by determining that carpal tunnel syndrome did not constitute a violation as it did not substantially limit the plaintiffs major life activities.

The Rights and Status of Gay Males and Lesbians

The "Stonewall Riot" in 1969, in which homosexuals clashed with police after a raid at a gay bar, created the movement for gay and lesbian rights. This movement has produced changes in state laws concerning sexual relations between consenting adults and, in some areas, has prompted special laws against gay and lesbian discrimination. The gay rights agenda was dealt a serious blow with the Supreme Court's decision in *Bowers v. Hardwick* (1986). In this case a closely divided Court ruled that the Constitution did not protect the rights of homosexuals to engage in consensual sexual activities, thus clearing the way for states to continue to enact and enforce laws that made homosexual relations a crime. The *Bowers* decision was overturned by the Supreme Court in *Lawrence v. Texas* (2003), when the Court ruled that consensual sexual activity between homosexuals was a liberty protected by the Fourteenth Amendment. The growth of the political activity of gay men and lesbians has not escaped the notice of politicians. Conservatives have generally been against gay rights, while liberals have supported gay rights. In 1997, President Clinton became the first sitting president to address a gay rights organization; he was also a leading force in developing the "Don't ask, don't tell" policy to allow gays and lesbians to have careers in the military. The most controversial aspect of gay rights today is likely same-sex marriage. The Hawaii Supreme Court took the first step in the controversy in the 1990s by interpreting its constitution as a protection of same-sex marriage in its state. The concern over whether this precedent might make its way to the mainland prompted Congress to enact the Defense of Marriage Act in 1996. This legislation defined marriage, for federal purposes, as the union of a man and a woman and allowed states to refuse to recognize the legitimacy of same-sex marriages performed in other states. While many states have enacted legislation limiting marriage to the union of a man and a woman, others, such as Vermont and Connecticut, have created a special category for homosexual relationships known as civil unions. The Massachusetts Supreme Court has ruled that civil unions don't go far enough, suggesting that same-sex couples have the right to marry. In 2006, the New Jersey Supreme Court followed suit by allowing the recognition of gay marriage. Views on the rights of homosexuals to marry and form families have ramifications on child custody and gay adoption.

The Rights and Status of Juveniles

Children have generally not been accorded the same legal protection as adults, based on the assumption that parents will provide for and protect their children. The Supreme Court has slowly expanded the rights of children in a wide range of situations. The Twenty-Sixth Amendment, ratified in 1971, granted the right to vote to citizens who are eighteen years old. The fact that eighteen-year-olds could be drafted and sent to fight and possibly die in Vietnam was a key factor in lowering the voting age. In civil and criminal cases, the age of majority—that is, the right to manage one's own affairs and have full enjoyment of civil rights— varies from eighteen to twenty-one years, depending on the state. State laws define the civil rights of children and can encompass parental liability for juvenile acts as well as custody rulings. In criminal cases, the assumption of common law is that children from seven to fourteen years cannot commit a crime because they are not mature enough to understand what they are doing. In the past decade a number of high-profile crimes committed by children have caused some state officials to consider lowering the age at which a juvenile may be tried as an adult and faced with adult penalties, including the death penalty.

KEY TERMS

affirmative action
busing
civil disobedience
civil law
civil rights
common law
criminal law
de facto segregation
de jure segregation
feminism
fertility rate
gender discrimination
grandfather clause
Hispanic

Latino
literacy test
majority
mandatory requirement
necessities
poll tax
reverse discrimination
separate-but-equal doctrine
sexual harassment
subpoena
suffrage
white primary

OTHER RESOURCES

A number of valuable supplements are available to students using the Schmidt, Shelley, and Bardes text. A list of suggested supplements is at the end of the chapter. Ask your instructor how to obtain these resources. One supplement is highlighted here, the American Civil Liberties Union.

E-MOCRACY EXERCISES

Direct URL: http://www.aclu.org/intlhumanrights/racialjustice/30087prs20070613.html
You are seeking the 06-13-2007 press release.

Surf Instructions
Log on to www.aclu.org
Place your arrow on "Issues" which is on the right hand side of the screen.
From the drop down menu, select "Human Rights."
Scroll through the articles to find " New ACLU Report Details Pervasive Racial Discrimination in America"and select the article titled, **"ACLU Calls State Department Report a 'Complete Whitewash.'"**

Study Questions
1. What do you think is the purpose of the 1994 International Convention on the Elimination of All Forms of Racial Discrimination?
2. Do you believe that the U.S. State Department has fulfilled its reporting requirements for the purposes of this treaty?
3. Is it reasonable to expect full honesty in any government's self-reporting?

PRACTICE EXAM
(Answers appear at the end of this chapter.)

Fill-in-the-Blank   Supply the missing word(s) or term(s) to complete the sentence.

1.   In _____, the Supreme Court upheld the constitutionality of slavery.

2.   The constitutional principle derived from the Fourteenth Amendment that permitted racial segregation was called the _____ _____ _____ doctrine.

3.   The solution to both *de facto* and *de jure* segregation of schools was _____.

4.   Martin Luther King, Jr.'s, philosophy of _____ included such tactics as demonstrations and marches.

5.   The _____ _____ _____ of 1964 was the most far-reaching civil rights bill in modern times.

6.   The _____ _____ _____ of 1965 outlawed discriminatory voter-registration tests.

7.   The lack of women in the top professional and business jobs is referred to as the _____ _____.

8.   The issue of _____ _____ was addressed in the case of *Bakke v. University of California Regents.*

9.   Initially, the Age Discrimination in Employment Act did not address the issue of _____ _____.

10. The reason for the lack of rights for children in our society is the presumption that children are protected by their _____.

True/False Circle the appropriate letter to indicate if the statement is true or false.

T   F   1.   The case of *Plessy v. Ferguson* upheld the doctrine of separate but equal.

T   F   2.   The Reconstruction statutes after the Civil War helped to secure civil rights for African Americans equal to those of whites.

T   F   3.   Concentration of minorities in defined geographic locations results in *de facto* segregation.

T   F   4.   The era of civil rights protests in the mid 1950s began with the boycott of public bus transportation in Montgomery, Alabama.

T   F   5.   The white primary was used in southern states to deny African Americans the right to vote.

T   F   6.   The Supreme Court's decision in *Bakke* declared all affirmative action programs unconstitutional.

T   F   7.   Affirmative Action is a policy to "level the playing field" for groups that have been discriminated against in the past.

T   F   8.   Individuals with AIDS are covered under the American with Disabilities Act of 1990.

T   F   9.   The Supreme Court ruled that consensual homosexual sexual relations are protected by the Constitution in *Lawrence v. Texas*.

T   F   10. If an individual is legally a minor, he or she cannot be held responsible for any contracts signed.

Multiple-Choice Circle the correct response.

1.   The *Dred Scott* case
   a.   freed the slaves in the South.
   b.   contributed to a more peaceful resolution of the slavery issue.
   c.   contributed to the inevitability of the Civil War.
   d.   provided full and equal citizenship for all African Americans.
   e.   created the separate-but-equal concept.

2.   The reconstruction statutes had the effect of
   a.   securing equality for African Americans.
   b.   doing little to secure equality for African Americans.
   c.   restructuring society to provide for greater equality of opportunity.
   d.   setting the stage for the Civil War.
   e.   providing for a stronger national government.

3.   The effect of *Plessy v. Ferguson* on racial segregation was to establish a(n)
   a.   "clear and present danger" principle to further integration.
   b.   pattern to outlaw segregation in the South.
   c.   pattern for racial integration throughout the country.
   d.   constitutional cornerstone of racial discrimination throughout the country.
   e.   equality of voting rights for African Americans.

4.   *De facto* segregation of school districts can come about through
   a.   residential concentration of minorities in defined geographical locations.
   b.   school boards drawing boundary lines to include only certain minority groups.
   c.   Supreme Court edicts.
   d.   a program of forced busing across district lines.
   e.   the use of federal troops.

5. Recent Supreme Court decisions on busing to integrate public schools have emphasized
    a. more busing to fully integrate schools.
    b. spending more money to attract minority students without busing.
    c. stronger court controls over local schools.
    d. more minority schools.
    e. less race-conscious policies to further integrate students.

6. Discrimination in most housing was forbidden by
    a. the Civil Rights Act of 1964.
    b. the Civil Rights Act of 1968.
    c. the Voting Rights Act of 1965.
    d. the Equal Housing Act of 1965.
    e. Title VII of the Civil Rights Act of 1964.

7. Besides voting rights, another key issue for the women's movement in the U.S. is
    a. world peace.
    b. social equality.
    c. economic equality.
    d. an Equal Rights Amendment.
    e. abortion rights.

8. The first woman elected to a leadership position in Congress was
    a. Sandra Day O'Connor.
    b. Susan B. Anthony.
    c. Francis Perkins.
    d. Jeannette Rankin.
    e. Nancy Pelosi.

9. Sexual harassment of women in the workplace is
    a. no longer prohibited by statute.
    b. prohibited by Title VII of the Civil Rights Act of 1964.
    c. considered "protective" legislation which the Supreme Court has ruled unconstitutional.
    d. considered a form of reverse discrimination against men.
    e. prohibited by the case of *Oncale v. Sundowner Offshore Services, Inc.*

10. The policy steps taken to overcome the present effects of past discrimination are referred to as
    a. affirmative action.
    b. legal justification.
    c. equalizing lawsuit.
    d. statutory worth.
    e. reasonable care.

11. Mandatory retirement rules
    a. were prohibited by the Civil Rights Act of 1964.
    b. were prohibited by the Civil Rights Act of 1991.
    c. were prohibited by an amendment to the Age Discrimination in Employment Act.
    d. still apply to most professions, including teaching.
    e. only apply to a few professions, such as firefighting.

12. The Americans with Disabilities Act requires
    a. the hiring of unqualified job applicants with disabilities.
    b. free public transportation for individuals with disabilities
    c. "reasonable accommodation" to the needs of persons with disabilities.
    d. free medical insurance for individuals with disabilities.
    e. coverage for carpal tunnel syndrome.

13. The ruling in the case of *Bowers v. Hardwick* in 1986 provided that
    a. same-sex individuals could legally marry.
    b. anti-gay legislation is unconstitutional.
    c. homosexual conduct between adults can be made a crime.
    d. special laws protecting gay and lesbian rights are constitutional.
    e. all sodomy laws are unconstitutional.

14. The case that overturned the decision of *Bowers v. Hardwick* was
    a. *Sutton v. American Airlines*.
    b. *Boy Scouts of America v. Dale*.
    c. *Lawrence v. Texas*.
    d. *Romer v. Evans*.
    e. *Kimel v. Florida*.

15. The first president to address a gay rights organization was
    a. President Truman.
    b. President Nixon.
    c. President Bush.
    d. President Clinton.
    e. President Reagan.

16. Child custody and adoption by gay men and lesbians is
    a. illegal in the United States.
    b. legal in all states.
    c. legal in 22 states.
    d. still being decided by the Supreme Court.
    e. constitutionally protected under Title VII of the Civil Rights Act of 1964.

17. The reason for the lack of protection of the rights of children is the presumption by our society and lawmakers that children
    a. need no protection.
    b. have all the laws necessary for their protection.
    c. do not need government interfering in their lives.
    d. are basically protected by their parents.
    e. are not considered citizens under the Constitution.

18. The aim of the juvenile court system is to
    a. punish the offending youths.
    b. hold the youthful offenders until they can be tried as adults.
    c. teach good human conduct.
    d. reform rather than punish the youthful offenders.
    e. teach a useful trade so the individuals can get jobs when they get out.

19. Zero tolerance policies in public school districts usually refer to
    a. cutting class.
    b. obscene dress.
    c. violent acts.
    d. failing standardized state exams.
    e. students over the age of eighteen.

Short Essay   Briefly address the major concepts raised by the following questions.

    a.   Explain the impact on education of the Supreme Court's decision in *Brown v. Board of Education of Topeka* and discuss what new problems the decision fostered.

b.   Explain the major issues of gender discrimination in the workplace.

c.   Examine the concept of affirmative action. Discuss the important Supreme Court cases defining this concept.

d.   Describe the current rights of juveniles in both civil and criminal areas.

ANSWERS TO THE PRACTICE EXAM

Fill-in-the-Blank

1.   *Dred Scott v. Sanford*
2.   separate-but-equal
3.   busing
4.   nonviolence
5.   Civil Rights Act
6.   Voting Rights Act
7.   glass ceiling
8.   affirmative action
9.   mandatory retirement
10. parents

True/False

1. T		3. T		5. T		7. T		9. T
2. F		4. T		6. F		8. T		10. T

Multiple Choice

1. c	5. e	9. b	13. c	17. d
2. b.	6. b	10. a	14. c	18. d
3. d	7. e	11. e	15. d	19. c
4. a	8. e	12. c	16. c	

Short Essay

An adequate short answer consists of several paragraphs that relate to concepts raised by the question. Always demonstrate your knowledge of the ideas by giving examples. The following represent major ideas that should be included in these short essays.

1.   Explain the impact on education of the Supreme Court's decision in *Brown v. Board of Education of Topeka* and discuss what new problems the decision fostered.

The concept of separate but equal from *Plessy v. Ferguson* was overturned.
The order to implement "with all deliberate speed" was used as a loophole by state officials to slow the pace of integration of schools.
School integration in Little Rock, Arkansas was blocked by use of the state's National Guard.
President Eisenhower federalized the Arkansas national guard and integrated schools in Little Rock.
De Jure segregation is illegal under the *Brown* decision.
De Facto segregation due to housing patterns is dealt with by busing to achieve integration.

2. Explain the major issues of gender discrimination in the workplace.

Title VII of the Civil Rights Act of 1964 prohibits gender discrimination in the workplace.
One major issue is sexual harassment. Sexual harassment has been extended to the employer who does nothing to stop sexual harassment by an employee through court decisions in *Faragher v. City of Boca Raton* (1998) and *Burlington Industries v. Ellerth* (1998).
A second major issue is wage discrimination. The Equal Pay Act of 1963 prohibits unequal pay for men and women doing the same job. Comparable worth is the concept that takes into account skill, effort, and responsibility to determine pay because traditional "women's" jobs pay less than traditional "men's" jobs. Women have a harder time getting high corporate positions because of the "glass ceiling."

3. Examine the concept of affirmative action. Discuss the important Supreme Court cases defining this concept.

*   Affirmative action is special consideration or treatment to disadvantaged groups in an effort to overcome present effects of past discrimination.
*   *Bakke v. University of California Regents* (1978) ruled on the concept of reverse discrimination against those who do not have minority status. The Court ruled that specific quotas are unconstitutional but affirmative action was constitutional.
*   *Hopwood v. State of Texas* (1996) ruled that race and other factors could not be used for determining admission to professional school. However, this was not the decision of the U.S. Supreme Court, but rather, a decision of a lower federal court.
*   The U.S. Supreme Court in 2003 ruled that the affirmative action program of the University of Michigan law school, in which race was one factor considered among many other factors in order to ensure a diverse student body, was constitutional.

4. Describe the current rights of juveniles in both civil and criminal areas.

*   Juveniles do not have the legal rights of adults because it is assumed that parents will protect their children.
*   The Supreme Court has ruled that children are "persons" under the meaning of the Bill of Rights, but may enjoy less protection in specific situations.
*   The rights of juveniles depend upon the age of majority. This concept refers to the age at which a person is entitled by law to manage his or her own affairs and have full civil rights. This varies from eighteen to twenty-one years old depending upon the state.
*   In civil cases, juveniles cannot be held responsible for contracts, unless it is for necessaries (things necessary for subsistence as determined by the court).
*   In criminal cases, juveniles have the same due process rights as adults, but usually do not face the same penalties. In common law, it is presumed that children under fourteen do not understand the nature of their crimes. Recent mass murders by children under fourteen at a school in Jonesboro, Arkansas have prompted some to reexamine the issue of when a child may be tried as an adult and receive adult punishment, even the death penalty.

Chapter 6
PUBLIC OPINION AND POLITICAL SOCIALIZATION

CHAPTER SUMMARY

Public opinion plays an important role in our political system. The experience of President George W. Bush clearly demonstrates this. While he has enjoyed widespread support for his war on terrorism, the public has expressed deep skepticism about his war in Iraq. His administration's failure to respond to this negative opinion resulted in the Democrats gaining majorities in both the House of Representatives and the Senate. In the 2008, public opinion about the foreclosure crisis led to the swift passage of a stimulus package. Two other presidents embody just how powerful public opinion can be. Opposition to the war in Vietnam was a factor in 1968 when President Lyndon Johnson declined to run for reelection. Public outcry over the scandal surrounding the 1972 Watergate break-in gave Congress strong support to initiate impeachment proceedings against President Richard Nixon.

Defining Public Opinion

Public opinion is defined as the aggregate of individual values or beliefs shared by some portion of adults. Public opinion is made known in a democracy by voting, responding to polls, participating in protests, and lobbying by interest groups. There are very few issues on which most Americans agree. When a large proportion of the public does appear to hold the same view on an issue, a consensus exists. If opinion is polarized between two quite different positions, divided opinion exists. (See Figure 6-1 and 6-2 for examples of these concepts.)

How Public Opinion is Formed: Political Socialization

The process by which individuals acquire political beliefs and opinions is called political socialization. The most important influence in this process is the family. Children have a strong need for parental approval and are very receptive to a parent's opinions. The clearest family influence is political party identification. Schools are also an important influence. Education seems to influence the level of activity in the political process. The more education a person receives, the higher his or her level of political activity. Friendships and associations in peer groups can influence political attitudes. Some individuals, known as opinion leaders, have the ability to influence others because of position, expertise, or personality. Additionally, as our society reaches the point at which the media permeate almost every aspect of American life, it is hardly surprising that the media have a major influence on public opinion. When events produce a long-term political impact, it is said that a generational, or cohort, effect results. For example, voters who grew up in the 1930s during the Great Depression (and thus during the Franklin D. Roosevelt administration) were likely to become Democrats. On the other hand, the election of Ronald Reagan in 1980 produced a period of economic prosperity that led many young people to identify with the Republican Party.

Political Preferences and Voting Behavior

A major indicator of voting behavior is political party identification. In addition, there are a variety of other factors that influence voting decisions. These include socioeconomic and demographic factors such as education, income and socioeconomic status, religion, ethnic background, gender, age, and geographic region. Those with a high school education are likely to identify with Republicans, those with college degrees may support either Democrats or Republicans, while those with postgraduate educations are likely to identify themselves as Democrats. Those with low incomes are likely to support a governmental role in the economy while those with high incomes tend to favor a more limited governmental role. At the same time, lower-income Americans tend to be more culturally conservative while those with high incomes are likely to endorse cultural liberalism. While the conventional wisdom holds that those with low incomes vote Democratic and those with higher incomes vote Republican, there is recent evidence that professionals and the extremely wealthy are leaning toward the Democratic Party. Religion is a complex factor to define as an influence. However, it can be said that those who define themselves as fundamentalists or evangelicals and those who attend any church services at least once a week are likely to vote Republican. A majority of those who attend church less than once a week vote Democratic. African Americans tend to support Democratic candidates. The Latino community tends to be somewhat divided, with many supporting the Democrats but

46

Cuban-Americans supporting Republicans. In recent years Latino's have swung largely to the Democratic tickets as Republicans championed immigration restrictions. The election of Ronald Reagan in 1980 evidenced a gender gap, in which women were more likely to vote for Democrats for president. This gap is still seen, to varying degrees, in elections today. In 2006, 55 percent of women favor Democrats versus 50 percent of men (see Figure 6-3). Finally, geography also plays a role in voting behavior. Those in the South, the Great Plains, and the Rocky Mountains tend to favor Republicans while those on the West Coast and in the Northeast favor Democrats. Election-specific factors include party identification, the image or perception of the candidate, and issues—particularly economic issues. A campaign uses this information to "microtarget" its candidate's political message to specific groups of voters. This technique attempts to tailor the message to a group's specific interests in order to "sell" the candidate and obtain that group's vote.

Measuring Public Opinion

One of the most common means of gathering and measuring public opinion is through the use of opinion polls. In the 1800s, newspapers and magazines used face-to-face straw polls to attract readers. In the 20th century, the *Literary Digest* developed modern techniques by mailing questionnaires to subscribers. In 1936, the magazine's poll predicted that Alfred Landon would defeat Franklin Roosevelt for President. Landon won only two states, demonstrating with force that polls are only as effective as the population that is surveyed. The most important principle in poll taking is accuracy, which is achieved by the random selection of a survey's respondents. If drawn from a truly random sample of opinions, a poll should be rather accurate. Gallup and Roper polls interview about 1,500 individuals to get within a margin of error of 3 percent. (See Figure 6-4 for the margins of error since 1936.) Public opinion polls are snapshots of opinions at a specific time on specific questions. The timing of the poll, a sampling error of interviewing too few people, and the wording of the question can all produce an inaccurate prediction of a political outcome.

Technology and Opinion Polls

During the 1970s, telephone polling began to dominate in-person polling. The ubiquitous and intrusive nature of the telemarketing industry, however, prompted many people to use call screening technology, to simply stop answering their phones. The introduction of new communications technologies such as the switch to cell phone only or internet based telephone services. These changes have undermined the ability of telephone pollsters to reach their audience. High non-response rates undercut confidence in poll results. The Internet has replaced the telephone as the latest polling technology, although many of these polls are unscientific and unreliable.

Public Opinion and the Political Process

Although Americans are divided into numerous ethnic, religious, and political groups, the American political culture binds us together with the core values of (1) liberty, equality, and property; (2) support for religion; and (3) community service and personal achievement. Another important aspect of public opinion is the trust that individuals express in the government and political institutions. Trust in political institutions has experienced a steady decline since 2001. (See Figure 6-5.) Public opinion about the confidence in various institutions in our society declined throughout the 1990s. The military and the church are the institutions that have the public's highest levels of confidence. (See Table 6-2.) While average citizens may have little confidence in some government institutions, they still turn to government to solve major problems. (See Table 6-3.) While the exact influence of public opinion on government policy cannot be measured, it appears that politicians who ignore public opinion run the great risk of defeat in the next election.

KEY TERMS

agenda setting	media
consensus	opinion leader
divided opinion	opinion poll
gender gap	peer group
generational effect	political socialization
lifestyle effect	political trust

public opinion   socioeconomic status
sampling error   Watergate break-in

OTHER RESOURCES

A number of valuable supplements are available to students using the Schmidt, Shelley, and Bardes text. A list of suggested supplements is at the end of the chapter. Ask your instructor how to obtain these resources. One supplement is highlighted here, the Gallup organization's Web site.

E-MOCRACY EXERCISES

Direct URL: http://www.gallup.com/Home.aspx

Surfing Instructions:
Log on to http://www.gallup.com/Home.aspx

Choose any survey/article from the front page and read it.

Study Questions
   e.   What is the primary research question in the selected survey?
   f.   Who is the targeted group of respondents?
   g.   What method of surveying was employed (face-to-face, telephone, written, combination)?
   h.   What were the results?
   i.   Do you believe that this use of public opinion polling was effective? Does it reveal a lot or a little?

PRACTICE EXAM
[Answers appear at the end of this chapter.]

Fill-in-the-Blank   Supply the missing word(s) or term(s) to complete the sentence.

1.   The aggregate of individual values and beliefs is _____ _____.

2.   When he and his party chose to largely ignore the public's growing dissatisfaction with their policies in Iraq, President _____ and the Republican party lost many congressional seats.

3.   _____ _____ is polarized between two quite different positions.

4.   When a large proportion of the American public express the same view on an issue, we say that a _____ exists.

5.   The _____ is the most important influence in political socialization.

6.   The _____ _____ is the term that describes the differences in issue orientation and voting behavior between men and women.

7.   One of the most common ways of gathering public opinion is the_____ _____.

8.   Roper, Gallup, and Crossley developed modern polling techniques to predict the total voting population by using _____ _____ with small samples of selected voters.

9.   The most important principle in sampling public opinion is _____, which is achieved through _____.

10. Public trust of government has steadily _____ since 2001.

True/False   Circle the appropriate letter to indicate if the statement is true or false.

T   F   1.   Adverse public opinion undermined George W. Bush's plan to reform Social Security.

T   F   2.   Children accept their parents' political values because of communication and receptivity.

T   F   3.   Peer groups play an important role in political socialization.

T   F   4.   Generational effects can result in long-lasting attachments to political parties.

T   F   5.   Quota sampling is a more accurate technique for public opinion than random sampling.

T   F   6.   During the 1960s and 1970s, political trust declined steeply.

T   F   7.   The government institution the public has the most confidence in today is the military.

T   F   8.   Election research suggests that policymakers are responsive to public opinion.

T   F   9.   Government decisions cannot be made by simply adding up individual desires.

T   F   10.   Well-defined public opinion tends to restrain government officials from taking intolerable actions.

Multiple-Choice   Circle the correct response.

1.   The aggregate of individual values or beliefs shared by some portion of adults is referred to as
    a.   political opinion.
    b.   propaganda.
    c.   public opinion.
    d.   an ideology.
    e.   special interest.

2.   General agreement among the citizenry on an issue is called
    a.   propaganda.
    b.   public opinion.
    c.   consensus.
    d.   political rhetoric.
    e.   tactical agreement.

3.   When public opinion is polarized between two quite different positions it is said to be
    a.   a consensus.
    b.   divided.
    c.   private.
    d.   in error.
    e.   converse.

4.   The most important influence on political socialization is
    a.   the peer group.
    b.   the family.
    c.   political events.
    d.   education.
    e.   political leaders.

5.   According to studies, which group is mostly likely to use media to form basic political beliefs?
    a.   the elderly
    b.   college graduates
    c.   high school students
    d.   women
    e.   middle-aged men

6. Political events such as the Iraq War tend to produce what are called
   a.   peer group influences.
   b.   social and economic influences.
   c.   opinion leader influences.
   d.   generational effects.
   e.   demographic influences.

7. Fundamentalist or evangelical Christians tend to support
   a.   Democrats.
   b.   Republicans.
   c.   Independents.
   d.   devout candidates.
   e.   no political parties at all.

8. The gender gap refers to the tendency of women to vote for
   a.   Ronald Reagan.
   b.   female candidates.
   c.   Republican presidential candidates.
   d.   Democrat presidential candidates.
   e.   Independent candidates.

9. The *Literary Digest* polling activities are an example of
   a.   modern polling techniques.
   b.   the use of exit interviews.
   c.   a non-representative sample.
   d.   telephone interviews.
   e.   quota samples.

10. The most important principle in accurate sampling is
    a.   a large sample.
    b.   choosing an issue in which consensus can be found.
    c.   randomness.
    d.   asking the right questions.
    e.   use of a computer.

11. Sampling error is the difference between the sample result and the
    a.   eligible voters.
    b.   likely voters.
    c.   true result.
    d.   biased result.
    e.   best result.

12. Push polls are
    a.   the most accurate opinion polls.
    b.   used by candidates to influence voters.
    c.   used by television reporters.
    d.   like quota sampling.
    e.   similar to telephone polls.

13. The most important values in the American political system include
    a.   federalism, unity, and freedom.
    b.   support for the president, Congress, and the courts.
    c.   liberty, equality, and property.
    d.   the two-party system and respect for the Constitution.
    e.   truth and justice.

14. Political trust in the United States has
    a.   increased since a low point during the Vietnam War.
    b.   slowly increased during the 1990s.
    c.   slowly decreased to a low point in 2003.
    d.   remained very steady over the last 30 years.
    e.   steadily decreased since 2001.

15. According to polls, the most trusted institution in the United States is
    a.   the church.
    b.   banks.
    c.   the U.S. Supreme Court.
    d.   television.
    e.   the military.

16. The Gallup Report of 2003 listed which of the following as the most important problems facing Americans?
    a.   morals, family decline
    b.   economy, education
    c.   terrorism, economy
    d.   crime, violence
    e.   budget deficit, recession

17. According to political scientists Page and Shapiro, the government responds to public opinion about
    a.   10 percent of the time.
    b.   30 percent of the time.
    c.   43 percent of the time.
    d.   66 percent of the time.
    e.   75 percent of the time.

18. Although people do not have much confidence in government institutions, polls show that they
    a.   expect government to solve major problems.
    b.   expect nonprofits to solve major problems.
    c.   expect individuals to solve major problems by dropping out of society.
    d.   avoid thinking about problems.
    e.   expect state government to solve all problems.

19. Which of the following statements about public opinion polls is correct?
    a.   Public opinion polls lead to direct policy change.
    b.   Public opinion polls do not identify issues important to the public.
    c.   Public opinion polls are not very important in the political process today.
    d.   Public opinion polls do identify issues important to the public.
    e.   Public opinion polls provide leaders with clear-cut policy decisions.

20. Which of the following statements about the effect of public opinion on the political process is correct?
    a.   Public opinion has almost the same effect as elections.
    b.   Public opinion may influence the president but not Congress.
    c.   Public opinion doesn't really affect political campaigns.
    d.   Public opinion polls are rarely paid for by politicians.
    e.   Public opinion is most important in preventing totally objectionable policies.

Short Essay   Briefly address the major concepts raised by the following questions.

1.   Define the qualities of public opinion.

2.   Describe the key factors in conducting opinion polls.

3.   Explain the most important influences in political socialization.

4.   Discuss the most important values of the American political system and the trends of political trust in the last three decades.

ANSWERS TO THE PRACTICE EXAM

Fill-in-the-Blank

1.   public opinion
2.   George W. Bush
3.   divided opinion
4.   consensus
5.   family
6.   gender gap
7.   opinion poll
8.   personal interviews
9.   accuracy randomness
10. declined

True/False

1. T	3. T	5. F	7. T	9. T
2. T	4. T	6. T	8. T	10. T

Multiple Choice

1. c	6. d	11. c	16. c
2. c	7. b	12. b	17. c
3. b	8. d	13. c	18. a
4. b	9. c	14. e	19. d
5. c	10. c	15. e	20. e

Short Essay

An adequate short answer consists of several paragraphs that discuss the concepts addressed by the question. Always demonstrate your knowledge of the ideas by giving examples. The following represent major ideas that should be included in these short essays.

1.   Define the qualities of public opinion.
The aggregate of individual values or beliefs shared by some portion of the adult population.
Consensus opinion is general agreement among the citizenry on an issue.
Divided opinion is public opinion that is polarized between two quite different positions.

2.   Describe the key factors in conducting opinion polls.
There are three key factors in conducting accurate public opinion polls:
Accuracy is the most important factor, achieved by randomness of the sampled population. The sample to be interviewed must be representative of the whole population. One technique is to choose a random sample of telephone numbers. A quota sampling, which is not as accurate, represents certain types of people. The major polls can interview about 1,500 people and predict elections within a margin of 3 percent, plus or minus.

Timing is a second factor. Polls continue to be conducted until the election day because a shift in opinion at the last minute can produce an unexpected outcome. The polls in the presidential election of 1980 between Carter and Reagan showed a very close contest. Reagan won easily, because of a shift in the undecided vote during the last week of the election.

The types of questions asked on the survey have a major impact on the results of the poll. If poorly worded or leading questions are asked, the results will be distorted.

3. Explain the most important influences in political socialization.
   - Political socialization is the process by which individuals acquire political beliefs and values.
   - The demographic factors of age, gender, location, and region of residence have an influence on the process we call political socialization.

The family is the most important influence and largely responsible for political party choice.

Party identification is the largest predictor of voting behavior.

Schools are most likely to influence the understanding of issues and political activity.

Peer groups most strongly influence direct involvement in political activity.

Religion has some impact on political activity, but its influence is not clear.

Wealth and social class can influence or increase one's tolerance for differences in voting activity.

Generational events, such as the Great Depression, can influence opinion for decades.

Charismatic opinion leaders using the power of media can have a tremendous impact on opinion.

4. Discuss the most important values of the American political system and the trend in political trust over the last three decades.

   The core elements of the American political system include:

Liberty, equality, and property.

Support for religion.

Community service and personal achievement.

These generally supported values provide an environment of support for the political system, which helps the system survive a crisis such as scandal. The levels of political trust that citizens express in the system declined tremendously in the 1960s and 1970s and reached an all-time low in 1992. The events of 9/11 inspired a greater level of political trust. The military and the Supreme Court are the most trusted institutions of the political system today.

Chapter 7
INTEREST GROUPS

CHAPTER SUMMARY

Interest groups have become a dominant force in American government and politics. To understand American government and politics at this point in time we must understand interest groups.

Interest Groups: A Natural Phenomenon

Alexis de Tocqueville observed in 1834 that America seemed to be a nation of joiners of associations. Interest groups are often created from mass social movements, which represent the demands of a large segment of the population for major social change. The civil rights movement of the 1950s and 1960s is a good example of a social movement that spawned a variety of interest groups, as is the women's suffrage movement. The pluralist theory discussed in Chapter One posits that the structure of American government invites a political process in which interest groups compete with one another and that governmental policy is to a great extent the product of this competition among interest groups. Competition by interest groups for access to lawmakers automatically checks the extent to which any one particular group can influence Congress. Finally, the First Amendment provides a solid constitutional foundation for the creation of interest groups.

Why Do Americans Join Interest Groups?

According to Mancur Olson, it may not be rational for individuals to join groups. If a group is successful in getting some benefit, how can that benefit be denied to others in the same situation? Why pay union dues, if workers' collective benefits achieved by the union go to all workers? It is more logical to wait for others to gain benefits and then share them. People need incentives to join groups, and the three major incentive categories are solidary, material, and purposive. Solidary incentives include companionship, a sense of belonging, and the pleasure of associating together. Material incentives are, of course, economic benefits or opportunities. Purposive incentives relate to one's ethical beliefs or ideological principles.

Types of Interest Groups

(See Table 7-1 for the 25 most effective interest groups; Table 7-2 lists other important groups.) Although thousands of groups exist to influence government, they can be discussed in a few broad categories. More interest groups are formed to represent economic interests than any other set of interests. Mirroring the complexity of the U.S. economy, these groups are various and include the interests of business, agriculture, labor, public employees, and professional organizations. The largest business groups are the National Association of Manufacturers and the U.S. Chamber of Commerce. American farmers have been very successful in lobbying for government support, even though they represent only 2 percent of U.S. workers. Farmers have obtained significant subsidies to insure the economic success of their products regardless of market costs. Their most recent 2002 Farm Bill is due for reauthorization in 2008. The American Farm Bureau and the National Farmers' Union are the most powerful agriculture groups. Labor unions have tried to balance the power of business groups but have weakened in recent years. The largest labor union is the giant AFL-CIO. (See Figure 7-1 for the decline and changes in union membership.) Unions are currently lobbying Congress to pass legislation that will make it easier to join a union, hoping to reverse this decline in membership. Public employee interest groups have grown in recent years. These groups are similar to labor unions but lack the legal power to strike, which has not always prevented them from actually doing so. One of the largest of these unions is the American Federation of State, County, and Municipal Employees. Finally, professions such as lawyers and doctors are well represented by the American Bar Association and American Medical Association, respectively. The poor are notably absent from the interest group system of politics even though they have strong economic concerns. Environmental interest groups began in the early part of the 20th century with the creation of the National Audubon Society and the Sierra Club. Since the 1970s and the first celebrated Earth Day, groups with mass memberships have increasingly arisen. These groups include the National Wildlife Federation and the Nature Conservancy. Public interest groups are concerned with some aspect of the public good. Two of the most significant public interest groups are

Common Cause and the American Civil Liberties Union. Ralph Nader has been very active in establishing public interest groups. Single interest groups can be very effective because they concentrate all of their resources on a single issue. The National Rifle Association is an example of this type of group. Finally, foreign governments—especially the largest trading partners of the U.S.—hire lobbyists to try to influence trade policy. Japan, South Korea, and Canada are just a few of the foreign governments seeking to influence policy.

What Makes an Interest Group Powerful?

There are four factors that have allowed interest groups to attain a reputation for being powerful: their membership size, which provides support for their cause; their financial resources, for obvious reasons; the effectiveness of their leadership (in strategizing, accessing power, and charisma); and cohesiveness of their membership, which speaks to members' motivation regardless of the group's financial resources.

Interest Group Strategies

The techniques used by interest groups can be divided into the direct and the indirect. The direct technique involves engaging in lobbying, publicizing interest group ratings of public officials, forming coalitions, and making campaign contributions. Lobbyists are private citizens (often with political pedigrees) who meet public officials on behalf of the interest that they represent. Lobbying activities include furnishing legislators with information, testifying before legislative committees and administrative agencies, assisting in the drafting of legislation and regulations, and socializing with legislators and government officials. Many groups will publish the voting records of legislators on issues of interest to the group. The indirect technique involves the use of the general public or individuals to influence the government for the interest group. Interest groups will try to generate a "groundswell" of support through mass mailing and advertising. Climate control is a similar concept, in which organizations will use public relations techniques to create favorable public opinion about a group or industry. Another effective indirect technique is the use of constituents to lobby the lawmaker. The "shotgun" approach is one in which the group tries to get as many people as possible to write, call, or e-mail legislators; the "rifle" approach tries to get a few influential constituents to talk to the lawmaker.

Regulating Lobbyists

The first attempt to regulate lobbyists and lobbying activities was the Legislative Reorganization Act of 1946, although judicial interpretation of the law resulted in very few lobbyists being required to register and comply with the law. In 1995, Congress enacted legislation designed to bring about significant reform in lobbying. This legislation expanded the definition of "lobbyist" to encompass more people, required registration of lobbyists, mandated disclosure regarding lobbying activities, and limited the ability of lobbyists to provide gifts to members of Congress. However, the revelation of extensive corruption by lobbyist Jack Abramoff, and his links with members of Congress, revealed that much more reform remains to be done. When the Democrats took control of Congress in 2007, one of its first undertakings was an attempt at ethics and lobbying reform. Legislation was signed into law requiring stricter enforcement of reporting laws that require lobbyist to disclose efforts that exceed $10,000 per quarter.

Interest Groups and Representative Democracy

The role of interest groups in our democracy is a continuing topic of debate. Members of interest groups have middle- or upper-class backgrounds. Leaders of interest groups have been called an "elite within an elite," because they are often part of a higher social class than the members of the group. Pluralist theory presumes that groups compete with one another for the benefit of the members; many critics, however, argue that interest group activity does not embody pluralism, but instead elite theory, as the most wealthy and influential gain the greatest benefit from the machinations of interest groups. In the overall analysis of interest groups, it is clear that even the most powerful group does not always prevail. By definition, an interest group can only be effective regarding a narrow range of interests that hold that group together. If the group tries to deal with broader policy issues outside those of its interest, the group will have little influence.

Key Terms

boycott
climate control
direct technique
free rider problem
indirect technique
interest group
labor movement
latent interests

lobbyist
material incentive
public interest
purposive incentive
service sector
social movement
solidary incentive

OTHER RESOURCES

A number of valuable supplements are available to students using the Schmidt, Shelley, and Bardes text. A list of suggested supplements is at the end of the chapter. Ask your instructor how to obtain these resources. One supplement is highlighted here, the AFL-CIO.

E-MOCRACY EXERCISES

Direct URL: (Takes you to the "choose your state" function.)
http://www.aflcio.org/issues/legislativealert/votes/vr_memb.cfm

Surfing Instructions:
Log on to www.aflcio.org
Type "Legislative Alert Center" into the "Search" field.
From the search results select "Legislative Alerts"
Click on "Congressional Voting Record" Located under "In this section" on the left side of the screen.
In the center of the page, click on "Voting Record By Member of Congress."
Choose your state from the map.
Pick your representative or one of your senators.

Study Questions
1. What influence do you think this record would have upon your member of Congress?
2. Does the voting record of your member of Congress indicate that he/she is a supporter of union interests?
3. Do you think this type of vote record monitoring is a good way to evaluate a member of Congress?
4. Go back to the map and select a member of Congress that represents Michigan. Why should you not be surprised that any Congressperson from Michigan will have a very positive union voting record?

PRACTICE EXAM
(Answers appear at the end of this chapter.)

Fill-in-the-Blank   Supply the missing word(s) or term to complete the sentence.

1. An interest group must give individuals an _____ to become members.

2. _____ _____ represent the demands of a large segment of the public for social change.

3. Numerous interest groups in the United States have been formed to promote _____ interests.

4. In spite of representing about 2 percent of the population, _____ interest groups have been very successful in receiving government aid.

5. Since 1965, the degree of unionization of the _____ sector has declined, but this has been offset by the growth of unionization of _____ employees.

6. Consumer activist _____ _____ has organized the most well known public interest groups.

7. The nation's largest interest group is the _____ .

8. The techniques used by interest groups may be divided into those that are _____ and those that are _____.

9. A recent scandal involving _____ focused attention on the need to continue to reform lobbying of members of Congress.

10. _____ _____ is a public relations strategy by an interest group to improve its public image.

True/False   Circle the appropriate letter to indicate if the statement is true or false.

T   F   1. The structure of our political system makes it difficult for individuals and groups to exert influence on the system.

T   F   2. James Madison was a firm believer in strengthening interest group activity.

T   F   3. The strength of union membership has traditionally been seen in the service sector of the workforce.

T   F   4. Foreign governments are prohibited from lobbying in the United States.

T   F   5. The use of public relations techniques to influence public opinion about a group is called the rifle approach.

T   F   6. One of the most effective interest group activities is the use of constituents to lobby for the group's goals.

T   F   7. The Federal Regulation of Lobbying Act regulates all forms of lobbying at the national level of government.

T   F   8. Most interest groups have a middle-class or upper-class bias.

T   F   9. The power of interest groups today is greater than ever before.

T   F   10. The existence of interest groups allows individuals to influence government far beyond just the votes they cast.

Multiple Choice   Circle the correct response.

1. Any organized group whose members share common objectives and actively attempt to influence the government is a(n)
    a. political party.
    b. bureaucracy.
    c. interest group.
    d. institution.
    e. social movement.

2. It is possible for individuals and groups to exert influence at many different points in our government because
    a. officials are always looking for campaign contributions.
    b. interest group members are also voters.
    c. of the structure of our political system.
    d. we have a unitary form of government.
    e. of mass social movements.

3. Companionship, a sense of belonging, and the pleasure of associating with others as reasons for belonging to interest groups are referred to as
    a. material incentives.
    b. purposive incentives.
    c. solidary incentives.
    d. herd incentives.
    e. lobbyist incentives.

4. Interest groups are often spawned by
    a. increases in young voters.
    b. publication of "underground" newspapers.
    c. factionalism.
    d. mass social movements.
    e. boycotts.

5. The role of labor unions in American society has weakened in recent years, as witnessed by
    a. the rise of business groups.
    b. a decline in union membership.
    c. the lack of effective leadership.
    d. an increase in government regulation.
    e. a lack of money.

6. Since 1965, the greatest growth in unionization has occurred in the unionization of
    a. military personnel.
    b. professional athletes.
    c. public employees.
    d. private sector employees.
    e. service sector employees.

7. The nation's largest interest group is
    a. AARP.
    b. Common Cause.
    c. the National Education Association.
    d. the National Rifle Association.
    e. the AFL/CIO.

8. Which of the following is NOT a special one-issue interest group?
    a. National Abortion Rights
    b. National Rifle Association
    c. The Right to Work Committee
    d. AFL-CIO
    e. American Israel Public Affairs Committee

9. Foreign governments are
    a. banned by the Constitution from lobbying in the U.S.
    b. banned by Congress from lobbying in the U.S.
    c. able to lobby extensively.
    d. able to lobby, but rarely do so.
    e. able to lobby, but only the largest nations do so.

10. Lobbying, ratings of legislative behavior, and campaign assistance are
    a. the main indirect techniques used by interest groups.
    b. considered ineffective methods of swaying votes.
    c. the main direct techniques used by interest groups.
    d. considered obsolete in view of today's modern technology.
    e. effectively regulated by national law.

11. Endorsements of an interest group are important to candidates because
    a. they usually bring campaign contributions.
    b. they can be used to attack the group's opponent.
    c. members of the group are sure to vote for the candidate.
    d. the candidate doesn't have to campaign as intensely.
    e. the candidate can use the endorsement in campaign advertising.

12. One of the benefits of forming alliances between interest groups is that
    a. it is easier to keep track of interest groups if they are fewer in number.
    b. it makes it easier to solicit contributions.
    c. it inevitably leads to success.
    d. it shares expenses and multiplies the influence.
    e. it confuses voters.

13. The "shotgun" approach to lobbying consists of
    a. mobilizing large numbers of constituents to write or phone their legislators.
    b. identifying specific constituents to write or phone their legislators.
    c. concentrating only on gun control issues.
    d. allowing lobbyists to determine the most appropriate strategy.
    e. spreading a lot of campaign money around.

14. The use of public relations techniques to create favorable public opinion toward an interest group is called
    a. lobbying.
    b. rating.
    c. climate control.
    d. groundswell.
    e. demonstration.

15. The *U.S. v Harriss* case ruled that the Federal Regulation of Lobbying Act of 1946
    a. was constitutional.
    b. was unconstitutional.
    c. should be left to the states to regulate.
    d. only applies to presidential elections.
    e. requires voluntary registration.

16. The recent changes of the Federal Regulation of Lobbying Act exempted what kind of lobbyist?
    a. lobbyists earning less than $200,000 a year
    b. "grassroots" lobbyists
    c. all lobbyists
    d. lobbyists spending 40 percent or less of their time lobbying
    e. lobbyists representing foreign-owned firms

17. Interest groups tend to have a(n)
    a. lower-class bias.
    b. middle- to upper-class bias.
    c. neutral bias.
    d. democratic foundation for decision making.
    e. mix of people from all economic classes.

18. The theory that views politics as a struggle among interest groups is
    a. elitism.
    b. democracy.
    c. pluralism.
    d. federalism.
    e. monopoly.

19. The advantage for democracy in interest group activity is that
    a. it is a way to demonstrate support for governmental policy.
    b. individual citizens are empowered to influence government.
    c. it serves as a basis for political party organization.
    d. it is a way to monitor the activities of Congress.
    e. it helps to pay for political campaigns.

Short Essay   Briefly address the major concepts raised by the following questions.

1. Discuss the incentives for an individual to join an interest group.

2. Describe the various types of major interest groups.

3. Explain the direct techniques used by interest groups to influence government.

4. Discuss the indirect techniques used by interest groups to influence government.

ANSWERS TO THE PRACTICE EXAM

Fill-in-the-Blank
1. incentive
2. social movements
3. economic
4. agricultural
5. private, public
6. Ralph Nader
7. AARP
8. direct, indirect
9. Jack Abramoff
10. Climate control

True/False

1. F	3. F	5. F	7. F	9. T
2. T	4. F	6. F	8. T	10. T

Multiple Choice

1.	c	6.	c	11.	e	16.	b
2.	c	7.	a	12.	d	17.	b
3.	c	8.	d	13.	a	18.	c
4.	d	9.	c	14.	c	19.	b
5.	b	10.	c	15.	a		

Short Essay

An adequate short answer consists of several paragraphs that relate to concepts addressed by the question. Always demonstrate your knowledge of the ideas by giving examples. The following represent major ideas that should be included in the short essay answer.

1. Discuss the incentives for an individual to join an interest group.

There are three major incentives for individuals to join interest groups: solidary, material, and purposive.

- Solidary incentives include companionship, a sense of belonging, and the pleasure of associating with others.
- Material incentives are economic benefits or opportunities, such as discounts, insurance, or travel planning.
- Purposive incentives provide the satisfaction of taking action for one's beliefs or principles.

2. Describe the various types of major interest groups.

The major types of interest groups are economic, environmental, public, special, and foreign government.

- Economic interest groups include business, agricultural, labor, public employees, and professional.
- Environmental interest groups began in 1905 with the National Audubon Society. More recently formed groups include The National Wildlife Federation and The Nature Conservancy.
- Public interest groups were greatly influenced by consumer activist Ralph Nader. One of the largest public interest groups today is Common Cause.
- Special interest groups, or single-interest groups, focus on one issue, for example they are either for or against abortion or gun control.
- Foreign governments that are major trading partners of the U.S. lobby for trade concessions and aid from the U.S. government.

3. Explain the direct techniques used by interest groups to influence government.

There are four important direct techniques of interest group influence: lobbying, rating of legislators, alliance building, and campaign assistance.

- Lobbying entails a range of activities that can include private meetings, testifying in public meetings, drafting legislation, providing political information, and influencing at social occasions.
- Rating of legislators on specific votes on issues important to the group provides the members of the group with important information on which candidates are sympathetic to the group's cause.
- When interest groups form alliances, they can share costs and multiply their influence.
- Campaign assistance can be provided in the form of endorsements and/or campaign contributions. The influence and dollar amount of the latter have grown tremendously in the past two decades.

4. Discuss the indirect techniques used by interest groups to influence government.

Indirect techniques allow interest groups to influence government policy in two ways: by using the general public and by using individual constituents.

- Interest groups try to create a "groundswell" of public opinion through using mass advertising. Sometimes, public relations techniques are used to create favorable public opinion toward the interest. This technique is known as climate control.
- The use of individual constituents is one of the most successful techniques. The attempt to mobilize as many constituents as possible is known as the "shotgun" approach. An attempt to mobilize very influential constituents is called the "rifle" approach.

Chapter 8
POLITICAL PARTIES

CHAPTER SUMMARY

Political parties: it takes little effort to join one, there are no membership cards or dues, and those who identify with (or, in the parlance, "belong to") one aren't actually obliged to do anything for that party. What, then, do we mean when we talk about a political party?

What is a Political Party?

A political party is a group of political activists who organize to win elections, operate the government, and determine public policy. It differs in goals and operation from both interest groups and factions. A faction is a group or bloc within a legislature or political party that is trying to obtain power or benefit. Political parties are umbrella organizations that may include multiple factions, either whole or partial. Political parties have five basic functions. These are: 1) recruiting candidates for public office, 2) organizing and running elections, 3) presenting alternative policies, 4) accepting responsibility for operating the government, and 5) acting as the organized opposition to the party in power.

A History of Political Parties in the United States

The evolution of our political party system can be divided into seven periods. The first period, from 1789 to 1816, featured the creation of political parties, with the Federalists and Anti-Federalists split over the ratification of the Constitution. After ratification the Federalists continued to advocate for a strong central government and focused on commercial interests, including merchants and large planters. Thomas Jefferson led the other party, which came to be known as the Republican Party (scholars tend to refer to it as the Democratic-Republican Party, to distinguish it from the Republican Party that would form at the time of the Civil War). This party represented the interests of farmers and artisans and while advocating states' rights. The second period, from 1816 to 1828, was referred to as the era of good feelings (or of personal politics), because elections centered on individual candidates rather than parties. It also saw the end of the Federalist Party. The third period spanned from 1828 to 1860 and featured the emergence of the Democratic Party, whose standard bearer was Andrew Jackson. This period also saw the creation and ultimately the demise of the Whig Party. Northern Whigs united with antislavery Democrats to form the Republican Party. The fourth period, from 1860 to 1896, featured a clash between the heavily Democratic South and the predominantly Republican North. The period from 1896 to 1932 saw the continued dominance of the Republican Party, although progressivism gained great influence and temporarily divided this party. From 1932 to about 1968, the nation went through the New Deal period, in which Democratic President Franklin Roosevelt created the basic landscape of politics that we have today. From 1968 to the present is the modern period, social issues began to predominate over economic concerns. The American voter in the last part of the 20th century gained an appreciation for divided government, in which one party controls the presidency while another party controls the Congress. As the new century began there was intense competition between the Democratic and Republican Parties. (See Figure 8-2 for a look at the 2004 election.) Since 2006 the electorate is increasingly voting for the Democratic Party.

The Two Major U.S. Parties Today

The core of the Democratic Party is made up of minorities, the working class, and various ethnic groups. Democrats generally support government intervention in the economy to help individuals in need. The Republican Party draws its support from college graduates, upper-income families, and professionals or businesspersons. Republicans support the private marketplace and feel that the government should be involved in fewer social programs. There are, however, significant areas of overlap and contradiction for both parties, as well as cultural, socioeconomic, and regional factors that make stereotyping more difficult. In the 2004 Presidential election, the Democrats tried to frame the election in terms of the economy, while the Republicans tried to focus on the issue of national security. In 2008, the Democratic Party's focus on the economy and healthcare led to electoral success.

The Three Faces of a Party

Each political party consists of three major components. The party-in-the-electorate includes the members of the general public who identify with a political party. The party organization includes the formal structure and leadership of a political party, including election committees; local, state, and national executives; and paid professional staff. The party-in-government includes all of the elected and appointed government officials who identify with a political party. American political parties are sometimes thought of as having a standard, pyramid-shaped organization, but it is more accurate to describe a party as having a confederal structure. The clearest institutional part of the national party organization is the national convention, which selects the national committee, nominates presidential and vice-presidential candidates, and develops the party platform. The party's presidential candidate chooses a national chairperson to lead the party. (For a look at the positions of national convention delegates in 2008, see Table 8-1.) The state party organization consists of a state central committee, state chairperson, and a number of local organizations. States parties are important in national politics because of the unit rule, which allots electoral votes in an indivisible bloc (except in Maine and Nebraska). The lowest level of party organization, called the grassroots, is composed of county and district party officials, precinct chairpersons, and party workers. The political machine that used to reward the grassroots party faithful is, for all practical purposes, extinct because of the decline of patronage. Local political organizations can still have a major impact on elections, particularly local elections. Finally, the party-in-government focuses on organizing and controlling the government. Americans historically have preferred to vote for divided government or to split the ticket between the two parties, which balances somewhat the power that a winning political party can exert through appointments. This type of power balance is contingent upon members voting strictly with their party. When party lines are crossed in Congressional voting, the balancing is not as effective.

Why Has the Two-Party System Endured?

There are a number of factors that explain why the United States has a two-party system. The development of the Federalists and Anti-Federalists early in our history established the foundation for two parties based on two distinct sets of interests. Political socialization of children to identify with the party of the parent has been an important factor in maintaining the two-party system. Our political culture has been one of consensus and moderation, which discourages radical third parties. The greatest portion of the electorate is ideologically grouped around the center of the political spectrum. The majority of Americans who vote, in general, do not hold extreme views either on the right or the left. The winner-take-all election system, particularly the Electoral College for electing the president, makes it very difficult for third parties to have any electoral success. Finally, most state and federal election laws provide a clear advantage to the two major parties. Third-party candidates for president are not eligible for federally matching funds.

The Role of Minor Parties in U.S. Political History

Though minor parties have not been able to compete successfully with the two major parties, they have played an important role in our political life. Ideologically based minor parties, such as the Socialist Party, had some electoral success in the early twentieth century. The most successful minor parties have been those that have split from the major parties. The Bull Moose Progressive Party in 1912 nominated Theodore Roosevelt for President, which created a three-way race and ultimately gave the election to Democrat Woodrow Wilson. (See Table 8-2 for the most successful third-party campaigns.) Additionally, minor parties have had an impact on American politics by raising important political issues that are then taken over by the two major parties. (See Table 8-3 for the policies of third parties.) In some notable cases, third-party candidates determine the outcome of the presidential election. The third-party candidate in 1992, H. Ross Perot, probably took votes away from Republican George Bush to give the victory to Democrat Bill Clinton. The third-party candidate in 2000, Ralph Nader, probably took votes away from Democrat Al Gore and opened the door for George W. Bush to win. In 2004, Nader ran as an independent and likely took votes away from Kerry, giving the election again to Bush.

Mechanisms of Political Change

To predict the future of the two U.S. parties, we can consider methods of past and ongoing political changes. Nationally, the Republicans dominated from 1896 to 1932, while the Democrats dominated from 1932 to 1968. A party can gain dominance through a realigning election. Realignment is a much-debated issue, as experts disagree about which elections indicate true partisan dominance and whether cycles of realignment can be predicted. Dealignment indicates a movement away from the two major parties. (See Figure 8-4.) Thirty-three percent of voters today classify themselves as independents, though a far smaller number of swing voters truly function independently at the ballot box. Within this independent group, at least one-third consistently vote Democratic and another one-third consistently vote Republican. Their declaration of "independence" may be more a personal psychological statement than a functional voting independence. The remaining one-third of independents are classified as swing voters and they truly switch their party votes on a consistent basis. A decrease in straight-ticket voting indicates that party loyalty is on the decline for all voters. Through tipping, the political landscape changes as demographics change; immigration is a prime tipping force. Speculation about the future must be tempered with the knowledge that unpredicted events can make any prediction obsolete.

KEY TERMS

dealignment
Democratic Party
divided government
Electoral College
era of good feelings
faction
independent
national committee
national convention
party identification
party-in-government
party-in-the-electorate
party organization
party platform
patronage

plurality
political party
realignment
Republican Party
reverse-income effect
splinter party
split-ticket voting
state central committee
straight-ticket voting
swing voters
third party
tipping
two-party system
unit rule
Whig Party

OTHER RESOURCES

A number of valuable supplements are available to students using the Schmidt, Shelley, and Bardes text. A list of suggested supplements is at the end of the chapter. Ask your instructor how to obtain these resources. One supplement is highlighted here, the Pew Research Center.

E-MOCRACY EXERCISES

Direct URL: http://typology.people-press.org/typology/

Surfing Instructions:
Log on to www.people-press.org
Click on "Where Do You Fit?"
Take the personal typology test and see what party bests fits your answers.

Study Questions
1. Are you surprised at the results?
2. Is this the same political party for which your parents vote?
3. In the summary results how do your personal beliefs differ from the category's description?

PRACTICE EXAM
(Answers appear at the end of this chapter.)

Fill-in-the-Blank   Supply the missing word(s) or term to complete the sentence.

1. A _____ _____ is a group of individuals who organize to win elections, to operate the government, and to determine public policy.

2. The first _____ political division in the United States occurred prior to the adoption of the Constitution.

3. The followers of Andrew Jackson created the _____ Party in 1828.

4. The major American political party that emerged in the late 1850s from the remains of the Whig Party was the _____ _____.

5. Each layer in the formal structure of a political party is virtually _____ from the other layers.

6. The real strength and power of a national party is at the _____ level.

7. Most minor parties that have endured have had a strong _____ foundation.

8. One of the myths of realigning elections was that they occurred every _____ years.

9. Dealignment is the _____ in political party loyalties.

10. When a group that is growing in population becomes large enough to change election outcomes, it is called _____.

True/False   Circle the appropriate letter to indicate if the statement is true or false.

T   F   1.   The party-in-the-electorate refers to those members of the general public who express a preference for one party over another.

T   F   2.   American political parties are tightly organized pyramid-shaped organizations with the national chairperson dictating policy to lower levels.

T   F   3.   The party platform is largely ignored once one of the two major parties captures control of the government.

T   F   4.   The national chairperson for each of the two major parties is actually chosen by their respective party's presidential nominee.

T   F   5.   The Federal Election Commission (FEC) rules for campaign financing place restrictions on minor party candidates.

T   F   6.   Virtually all levels of government in the United States use the plurality, winner-take-all electoral system.

T   F   7.   Minor parties have not played an important role in American politics.

T   F   8.   Beginning in 1860, realigning elections have occurred every 36 years.

T   F   9.   It appears that the electorate is increasingly voting a straight ticket.

T   F   10. The Democratic Party was formed around Abraham Lincoln.

Multiple Choice   Circle the correct response.

1.   The main feature differentiating a faction from a political party is that a faction
     a.   is composed only of conservatives, while a political party may have both liberals and conservat
     b.   generally does not have a permanent organized structure.
     c.   works best if there are competing factions in opposition to it.

    d.   helps to extend democracy to the rank-and-file party member.

    e.   has more money available to fund its operations.

2.   Political parties in the United States tend to perform all of the following activities EXCEPT

    a.   recruit candidates for public office.

    b.   organize and run elections.

    c.   act as the organized opposition to the party in power.

    d.   establish a large cadre of highly disciplined dues-paying party members.

    e.   present alternative policies to the electorate.

3.   The first two opposing groups in United States politics were the

    a.   Democrats and Republicans.

    b.   Federalists and Anti-Federalists.

    c.   Washingtonians and Jeffersonians.

    d.   Independents and Whigs.

    e.   Democrats and Monarchists.

4.   The era from 1816 to 1828, when attention was centered on the character of the individual running for office rather than on party identification, is referred to as

    a.   the "era of good feelings."

    b.   factional politics.

    c.   the "personal is political" age.

    d.   democratic politics.

    e.   free soil politics.

5.   After the end of the Civil War, the _____ became heavily Democratic and the _____ became heavily Republican.

    a.   North, South

    b.   South, North

    c.   East, West

    d.   West, East

    e.   East, South

6.   Since 1968, the modern party system has been

    a.   Republican-dominated.

    b.   Democrat-dominated.

    c.   complicated by strong third parties.

    d.   evenly divided between Republicans and Democrats.

    e.   dealigned due to voters choosing independent candidates.

7.   Since the presidency of Franklin D. Roosevelt, the core of the Democratic Party has been

    a.   middle-class, working Americans.

    b.   upper-class liberals.

    c.   minorities, the working class, and ethnic groups.

    d.   middle to upper-class Protestants and independents.

    e.   white evangelical Christians.

8.   The main purpose of the national party conventions every four years is to

    a.   nominate the presidential and vice-presidential candidates.

    b.   write a party platform.

    c.   check the credentials of all party activists.

    d.   develop a strategy for the upcoming presidential election.

    e.   conduct party business.

9.   In terms of party organization, the real strength and power of the Democratic and Republican parties

    a.   resides with their members in the U.S. Congress.

b. is determined by their national committee chairpersons.
c. resides at the state level of party organization.
d. is determined by the number of election victories each party has in a given time period.
e. is determined by the "grassroots."

10. The principal organized structure within states for each political party is the
    a. precinct committee.
    b. ward captain.
    c. state central committee.
    d. governor's council.
    e. elected members of state government.

11. Rewarding members of a political party with government jobs and/or contracts is known as
    a. bribery.
    b. graft and corruption.
    c. non-competitive bidding.
    d. patronage.
    e. strategic planning.

12. The most successful minor parties have been those that have
    a. focused on the positive things in life, not the negative.
    b. been formed from the break-up of the Democratic party prior to WWI.
    c. split from major parties.
    d. opposed the existing economic power structure.
    e. spent the most money.

13. The most important reason spurring the creation of splinter parties is
    a. ideology.
    b. class politics.
    c. a particular political personality.
    d. the U.S. political culture.
    e. dealignment.

14. The third party that may possibly have cost Democrat Al Gore the presidency in the 2000 election was the
    a. Green Party.
    b. Reform Party.
    c. Socialist Party.
    d. Libertarian Party.
    e. Peoples Party.

15. Independent voters in the 2000 presidential election made up _____ percent of the electorate.
    a. 25
    b. 33
    c. 40
    d. 50
    e. 55

16. Which of the following statement about party identification is true?
    a. In recent years, Democrats have increased, while Republicans and Independents have decreased.
    b. In recent years, Independents have increased, while Democrats and Republicans have decreased.
    c. In recent years, Republicans have increased, while Democrats and Independents have decreased.
    d. In recent years, Democrats, Republicans, and Independents have decreased.
    e. In recent years, a majority of people would not give a party identification.

17. Truly independent voters in elections are called
    a. independents.
    b. leaners.
    c. swing voters.
    d. tippers.
    e. straight voters.

18. A change in population in certain areas that alters the political landscape is referred to as
    a. swing voting.
    b. straight-ticket voting.
    c. tipping.
    d. leaning.
    e. dealignment.

19. Calling the U.S. a two-party system is an oversimplification because
    a. a third-party candidate almost won the 2000 presidential election.
    b. the nature and names of the two major parties have changed over time.
    c. ideology is such an important factor in U.S. elections.
    d. third parties receive public funding equal to that of the major parties.
    e. third parties can affect the political process even if they do not win.

Short Essay   Briefly address the major concepts raised by the following questions.

1. Distinguish between a political party and a faction. What are the basic functions of a political party?

2. Trace the evolution of political party development within the United States.

3. Identify the formal structure of political party organization in America.

4. Discuss the reasons for the two-party system in the United States.

ANSWERS TO THE PRACTICE EXAM

Fill-in-the-Blank
1. political party
2. partisan
3. Democratic
4. Republican Party
5. autonomous
6. state
7. ideological
8. thirty-six
9. decline
10. tipping

True/False

1. T	3. F	5. T	7. F	9. F
2. F	4. T	6. T	8. F	10. F

Multiple Choice.

1. b	6. d	11. d	16. b
2. d	7. c	12. c	17. c
3. b	8. a	13. c	18. c
4. a	9. c	14. a	19. e
5. b	10. c	15. b	

Short Essay Briefly address the major concepts raised by the following questions.

1. Distinguish between a political party and a faction. What are the basic functions of a political party?

A political party is a group of political activists who organize to win elections, to operate the government, and to determine public policy.
Factions are smaller groups that may exist within political parties or a legislature who try to obtain power or certain benefits for themselves.
The basic functions of a political party are:
Recruiting candidates for public office.
Organizing and running elections.
Presenting alternative policies to the electorate.
Accepting responsibility for operating the government.
Acting as the organized opposition to the party in power.

2. Trace the evolution of political party development within the United States.

The formation of political parties in the U.S. went through seven basic periods. These are 1) the creation of parties, 2) the era of good feelings, 3) the period of the Jackson Administration to the Civil War, 4) the post-Civil War period, 5) the progressive period, 6) the New Deal period, and 7) the modern period.
- The first parties were created from 1789 to 1816 around support for ratifying the Constitution, with the Federalists for ratification and the Anti-Federalists opposed.
- From 1816 to 1828, voters focused on the candidates rather than the parties.
- From 1828 to 1860, political parties tended to focus on Andrew Jackson, and the Democratic and Whig parties developed.
- The post-Civil War period of 1860 to 1896 created our current two-party system, as the anti-slavery Republican Party was created.

- The Progressive era from 1896 to 1932 led to the split in the Republican Party and the 1912 election of the Democrats, who then proceeded to enact much of the Progressive Party platform.
- The New Deal programs of President Franklin D. Roosevelt, which established the current political landscape of the political party system, ushered in a Democratic ascendancy that lasted from 1932 to 1968.
- The modern era of divided government dates from 1968 to the present. The nation is almost evenly divided in politics, with one party generally winning the Presidency but losing the Congress, and vice versa.

3. Identify the formal structure of political party organization in America.

The formal political party organization structure consists of the national level, the state level, and the local level.
The national party organization holds a national convention every four years. At this convention, the party selects its candidates for president and vice president, writes a party platform, and selects a national committee. A national chairperson is selected by the presidential candidate and may be changed by the party if the candidate loses.
- The state central committee will carry out the decisions of the state party convention and, in some states, direct the activities of the state chairperson.
- The local party organization, called the grassroots, uses county committees and their chairpersons to direct and assist the activities of precinct leaders.

4. Discuss the reasons for the two-party system in the United States.

The historical foundations of the two-party system developed around relatively distinct sets of issues.
The first of these issues was ratifying the Constitution, which spawned the Federalists and Anti-Federalists.
Political socialization, in which parents influence their children's choices of political party, bolsters the two-party system.
The American political culture emphasizes a commonality of goals, which by necessity makes the two parties broad and able to accommodate different viewpoints.
The winner-take-all election system makes it very difficult for third parties to win elections.
State and federal election laws make it difficult for third parties to get on the ballot.

Chapter 9

CAMPAIGNS, ELECTIONS, AND THE MEDIA

CHAPTER SUMMARY

Free elections are the cornerstone of the American political system. By examining the election process, from candidates to campaign finance to casting votes, we can explore its strengths and weaknesses.

Who Wants to Be a Candidate?

People who run for political office fall into two groups: those who are self-starters and those who are recruited. There are few constitutional requirements to run for federal office. To serve as president, a candidate must be a natural-born citizen, age 35 or over, and a resident of the U.S for fourteen years when sworn in. For vice president, the requirements are the same as that of the president, plus the vice president cannot be a resident of the same state as the president. To run for the Senate an individual must have been a U.S. citizen for nine years, be at least 30 years old, and be a resident of the state from which he or she is elected. To run for the House of Representatives, a person must have been a citizen of the United States for seven years, be at least 25 years old, and be a resident of the state from which he or she is elected. While these requirements are minimal, most current office holders are white males due to past discrimination and a general inclination to resist change. Yet the number of women running for—and winning seats in—Congress is on the increase. (See Figure 9-1.) Most candidates elected to office tend to be professionals, especially lawyers.

The Twenty-First-Century Campaign

American political campaigns are extravagant, lengthy events with costs that run into millions, if not hundreds of millions, of dollars. To run a successful campaign the candidate's organization must be able to raise funds, obtain coverage from the media, produce and pay for political commercials and advertising, schedule the candidate's time effectively, convey the candidate's position on the issues to the voters, conduct research on the opposing candidates, and get voters to the polls. At one time a campaign was the work of volunteers and party political advisers, but with the rise of television in the 1960s, a candidate's public image became very important. Today candidates must make use of paid professionals, including political consultants and media strategists. These advisors use opinion polls and focus groups to gauge their client politician's public position. Additionally, because fewer voters identify strongly with the two main political parties, campaigns now place more emphasis on a candidate's policies and character than on his or her political affiliation.

Financing the Campaign

The tremendous cost of political campaigns has caused concern among the public and led Congress to pass a number of laws in an attempt to regulate campaign financing. In 1925, the Corrupt Practices Acts were passed, but they proved largely ineffective. The Hatch Act of 1939 attempted to limit spending by political groups but was also easily evaded. The Federal Election Campaign Act of 1972 (and its further reforms in 1974) essentially replaced all past laws and instituted a major reform. These laws created the Federal Election Commission (FEC), provided public funding for presidential elections, put limits on presidential spending, limited campaign contributions, and required funds disclosure by candidates. The Supreme Court considered the constitutionality of the limitations created by this law in *Buckley v. Valeo* (1976). The Court concluded that while limits on campaign contributions were constitutional, limits on a candidate's campaign spending violated the First Amendment. In the wake of this legislation lawyers and politicians devised strategies to evade it, including political action committees (PACs), "soft money" contributions, independent expenditures, and issue advocacy advertising. Since campaign spending could not be limited, PACs were formed to raise money and spend it on campaigns. Even though the money is never actually contributed to a candidate, and thus remains constitutional, it is spent in a manner that benefits the candidate. (See Table 9-1 for information on PAC contributions.) Soft money stayed on the good side of the Constitution because it is given to political parties rather than directly to candidates (though it ultimately works for the benefit of the latter). Through these independent expenditures, businesses, unions, and interest groups found that they could spend large amounts of money on a campaign as long as their expenditures did not coordinate with those of the candidate or political party. This kind of issue advocacy, in which the money is again not directly entering a candidate's coffer but is still being used to run ads that benefit the candidate, is becoming more common. The Bipartisan Campaign Reform Act of 2002 attempted to limit the use of campaign ads by outside special interest groups advocating the election or defeat of specific candidates. It also banned soft money contributions to the national political parties (but not to state or local parties). The 2002 Act limits an individual's contribution to $2,000 for each federal candidate's campaign. The individual is also limited to $95,000 in contributions to all federal candidates over a two-year election cycle. Although the Supreme Court upheld the constitutionality of the Campaign Finance Reform Act, interpretations of the law by the FEC diminished much of its effectiveness. Interest groups reacted to the latest legislation by creating "527" organizations. This name comes from the tax code that allows for the creation of a tax-exempt organization. Relying almost entirely upon soft money, 527s spend hundreds of millions of dollars to influence the outcome of elections via issue advocacy and targeted voter registrations. (See Table 9-2 for 527 activity in 2005-2006.)

Running for President: The Longest Campaign

The American presidential campaign has two phases. Traditionally, the first begins in January with the initial presidential primary (which can be run as a closed, an open, or a blanket primary, depending on who is allowed to vote) and ends in the summer with the party's national convention. The second phase usually begins on Labor Day and culminates with the presidential election in November. This ten-month process is lengthening due to the growing trend of states holding their primaries earlier in the year. After the riots at the 1968 Democratic National Convention prompted major changes in the primary election system, presidential candidates realized that the primary elections could be a springboard to win the presidency. If a candidate wins the first caucus in Iowa and the first primary in New Hampshire, he or she is likely to be labeled a front-runner by the media and receive a campaign boost. At this time, other states, attempting to get media coverage and increase their influence in the presidential nomination process, began to move up the day of their primary elections in a process known as front-loading. The national convention is the end result of all the state primary elections. A credentials committee determines which delegates may participate in the convention. In recent years, the delegates selected in the primaries have already given the nomination to a candidate before the convention begins. This has lessened the interest in and media coverage of the national convention. An additional body that influences who becomes president is the Electoral College, a group framed specifically by the Constitution. There are 538 total electors today, apportioned to states based on each state's representation in Congress and elected in each state in accordance with that state's law. Electors are not required to vote in accordance with the popular vote of their states, but they customarily do, awarding all of a state's electoral votes to the candidate taking a plurality of the popular vote. This has spawned criticism of the college. Also contentious is the argument that small states with low electoral vote numbers can be ignored in campaigns and its opposite viewpoint, that small states are actually overrepresented by being given three electoral votes in spite of their small populations. To abolish the Electoral College would require a constitutional amendment whose adoption is unlikely; reform, however, could be accomplished through legislation.

How Are Elections Conducted?

The United States uses the secret or Australian ballot, which is prepared, distributed, and counted by government officials at public expense. There are two types of ballots: the office-block, which focuses on the office rather than the party; and the party-column, which focuses on the party rather than the office and can encourage the straight-ticket vote and coattail effect. Though absentee voting has been conducted by mail for decades, mailed regular ballots have only been available recently. Oregon has abandoned polling places entirely and has seen increased voter turnout and decreased election cost. Experts are divided, however, on whether voting by mail increases participation or only increases the opportunity for vote fraud and mistakes. Vote fraud is often suspected but difficult to prove, whether it is alleged against unscrupulous political activists, phony voters, or corrupt election officials. Voting mistakes are problems with poorly designed ballots, outdated or malfunctioning voting equipment, along with questionable behavior by polling officials to disqualify voters or their votes. Studies have shown that disenfranchisement in recent years has disproportionately affected African Americans. In 2002, Congress passed the Help Americans Vote Act in an attempt to address some of these problems.

Turning Out to Vote

Voter turnout in the United States for the 2006 presidential election was only 40 percent of eligible voters. There are two reactions to the decline of voter turnout in the U.S. One is that the decline in voting turnout is a threat to our democracy. The other is that people are basically satisfied with the status quo and that is why they don't vote. Studies show that there are a number of factors that influence voter turnout, including age, education, minority status, income, and two-party competition. Voters tend to be older, more educated, non-minorities, wealthy, and more involved where there is two-party competition. (See Figure 9-2 and Tables 9-3, 9-4, 9-5, and 9-6 for information on turnout.) There are many explanations for why people may not vote, including uninformative media coverage, negative campaigning, and the rational ignorance effect, in which people decide not to spend the time and energy required to become informed voters. In research, 68 percent of non-voters cited a personal lack of information about the candidates as one of their reasons for not voting. Plans to improve voter turnout have focused on ways to make voting easier—such as simplified voter registration, voting by mail or through the Internet, or in advance of election day—but none have succeeded so far.

Legal Restrictions on Voting

Historically only white males who owned property were allowed to vote; the Constitution left suffrage questions to the states. Since the Civil War, constitutional amendments, such as the Fifteenth, Nineteenth and Twenty-Sixth, and acts of Congress, such as the Voting Rights Act, have gradually extended the right to vote. There are still certain classes of people who do not have suffrage, including noncitizens and convicted felons. Of the one-fifth of the eligible population who are not registered to vote, 20 percent are Democrats and 14 percent are Republicans. Currently, voting requires registration, and some scholars believe that even the minimal requirements of citizenship, age, and residency that make up the process of registration keep some people from voting.

The Media and Politics

Though the print media developed our understanding of how news should be reported, television is now the primary source of news for more than 90 percent of Americans. In the U.S., we can list six functions of the mass media, almost all of which have political implications, some to the point of necessity to the modern political process. These functions are as follows: 1) providing entertainment, by far the largest function; 2) reporting the news; 3) identifying public problems, thus setting the public agenda; 4) socializing new generations; 5) providing a political forum for leaders and the public; and 6) making profits, which come from advertising revenues and can be directly related to circulation or ratings. The relationship among media outlets, the government, and the public is complex.

The Primacy of Television

Television is big business; large audiences command high prices for advertising spots. Network news programming constituted about three hours each day by 2007, up from eleven minutes in 1963. Television is still constrained by time limitations, forcing news to be reported in sound bites or with clear "plots" and exciting pictures. It has been suggested that the format necessities of television increase its political influence unduly, as real life is rarely as dramatic, well-plotted, or discreet as television news might suggest. Sensational news is often reported ("if it bleeds, if leads") while more mundane items that are still newsworthy are not presented to the public.

The Media and Political Campaigns

Since all forms of media have significant political impact in America, it is not surprising that almost all political figures, from the president on down, carefully plan every appearance and statement with the media's coverage in mind. Television provides the main vehicle for campaign coverage in three ways: political advertising, management of news coverage, and campaign debates. Negative advertising, despite the public's dislike for it, is effective and nearly ubiquitous. Further, campaign staffers seek to control their candidate's image by understanding and finessing the presentation of that candidate and ensuring that a news organization gets a good, interesting story and interprets it correctly. Because interpretation can be influenced for good or ill, the spin put on a given story is so important that it warrants its own staffer, a spin doctor, to show campaign events or election results in the most advantageous light. Televised debates are a direct vehicle for a candidate's message. Challengers have more to gain in debates than do incumbents, and "image" is key. The Internet is growing in importance for political campaigns, both though official campaign presence on the Web and through affiliated and unaffiliated blogs. Every major political campaign now dedicates staff for the management of a campaign website. These sites provide easy access to video clips, speeches, policy stances, and most importantly, are powerful ways to raise campaign donations. Podcasting and sites such as YouTube also pose a threat to the mainstream media; along with blogs, these technologies can be cheap, easy, specialized, and entertaining. These Internet sources can also be detrimental to a candidate's ability to control his/her campaign's message. A verbal misstep becomes YouTube's latest download and bloggers may easily and instantly misrepresent a candidate's political stance. The ultimate influence of media on voters is difficult to determine, but since people view news and ads with selective attentiveness, the media apparently have the greatest pull over those who have not formed opinions about candidates or issues.

Government Regulation of the Media

Chapter 4 discussed many aspects of media regulation. Recall the Federal Communications Commission (FCC), which presides over communications by radio, television, wire, and cable. Many FCC rules have dealt with ownership of news media, but in 1996 Congress passed the Telecommunications Act, which not only opened the door to competitors for services like local and long-distance telephony, cable or satellite television, and Internet services, but also allowed competing companies to consolidate control over all such services. Many media outlets are now owned from top to bottom by corporate conglomerates. The FCC restrictions on the level of "audience reach" allowed to any one conglomerate—upped to 45 percent in recent years—were curtailed by Congress and knocked down to 40 percent, though it is still permissible for a single company to own up to three TV stations in its largest market. Such media concentration is a detriment to the presentation of local news. The government occasionally steps in to control media content. Supreme Court decisions have permitted the FCC to levy fines against broadcasters for profanity or indecency. Coverage of the Second Gulf War was facilitated by George W. Bush's Administration with the goal of avoiding the criticisms lodged against his father's actions in the First Gulf War. In the wake of the September 11, 2001 attacks, more and more government documents have been kept from the public in the name of national security, but the media have found several notable leaks, to public outcry. All these regulations circle an ultimate question: does the public have a right to media access? The actions of the FCC and the courts would seem to answer in the affirmative, and the Internet promises to expand access further (at least to those with the resources to take advantage of that promise).

Bias in the Media

It has been argued for decades that, speaking broadly, the media has a liberal bias. Eric Altman suggests that on the whole the media actually has a conservative bias, especially on economic issues. He also points to the near total conservative domination of radio talk shows. The emergence of blogs is still a relatively new force in politics and it has yet to be determined if there is a general bias within that aspect of the media.

KEY TERMS

Australian ballot	open primary
"beauty contest"	party-column, or Indiana ballot
bias	podcasting
caucus	political action committee (PAC)
closed primary	political consultant
coattail effect	presidential primary
corrupt practices acts	public agenda
credentials committee	rational ignorance effect
elector	registration
focus group	soft money
front loading	sound bite
front runner	spin
Hatch Act	spin doctor
independent expenditures	superdelegate
issue advocacy	tracking poll
office-block, or Massachusetts ballot	voter turnout

OTHER RESOURCES

A number of valuable supplements are available to students using the Schmidt, Shelley, and Bardes text. A list of suggested supplements is at the end of the chapter. Ask your instructor how to obtain these resources. One supplement is highlighted here, fairvote.org.

E-MOCRACY EXERCISES

Direct URL: http://www.fairvote.org/e_college/reform.htm

Surfing Instructions:
Log on to www.fairvote.com
In the Search box on the right, type "reform Electoral College."
From the search results select the article about "The Electoral College—Reform Options."

Read the short articles.

Study Questions
1. What are the suggested reforms for the Electoral College?
2. What specific problem is each reform attempting to address?
3. If a state has a relatively small population, why would it be threatened by a switch to popular voting?

PRACTICE EXAM

(Answers appear at the end of this chapter.)

Fill-in-the-Blank   Supply the missing word(s) or term to complete the sentence.

1. Candidates who run for office are described as either self-starters or those who are _____.

2. In terms of characteristics, holders of political office in the U.S. are overwhelmingly _____ and _____.

3. In the last three decades, campaigns have changed from volunteer campaign managers to paid _____ _____.

4. Campaign contributions banned by the Bipartisan Campaign Act of 2002 are referred to as _____ _____.

5. Each state's number of electors in the Electoral College equals the state's number of _____ plus its number of _____ in the U.S. Congress.

6. A(n) _____ ballot is a form of general election ballot in which the candidates are arranged by the office for which they are running.

7. Citizenship, age, and _____ are key requirements to register to vote.

8. The limits placed on spending were declared unconstitutional in the case of _____.

9. A _____ _____ is a brief, memorable comment that can easily be fit into news broadcasts.

10. _____ are threatening to mainstream media because they can be specialized, political, entertaining, and cheap.

True/False   Circle the appropriate letter to indicate if the statement is true or false.

T   F   1. Today, when campaigning for public office, candidates depend more and more on the resources of political parties.

T   F   2. Political campaigns are getting longer and more expensive each year.

T   F   3. Tracking polls are used by the government to keep track of campaign contributions.

T   F   4. The purpose of instituting the primary election was to open the nomination process to ordinary party members.

T   F   5. States began to change the dates of primaries to have more influence in nominating presidential candidates, in a process known as front loading.

T   F   6. The framers of the Constitution favored the selection of the president and vice president by the masses.

T   F   7. The use of mail-in ballots are seen as one way to increase voter turnout.

T   F   8. The media are not dependent on revenues from advertising to make profits.

T F 9. The public responds favorably to most attack ads.

T F 10. A challenger for public office has more to gain from participating in a public debate than does an incumbent politician.

Multiple Choice Circle the correct response.

1. The constitutional qualifications for the office of president include which of the following?
  a. 25 years of age
  b. 50 years of age
  c. natural-born citizen
  d. registered voter
  e. 20 years of government service

2. Which of the following characteristics is NOT descriptive of a professional campaign?
  a. increased length of the campaign
  b. use of paid political consultants
  c. increased costs of the campaign
  d. increased use of volunteers
  e. increased use of technology

3. The first attempt by Congress to regulate campaign spending was seen in the
  a. Hatch Act.
  b. Corrupt Practices Acts.
  c. CREEP Act.
  d. Federal Election Campaign Act.
  e. Bipartisan Campaign Act.

4. The purpose of the Federal Election Commission is to
  a. create an aura of good feeling in federal elections.
  b. oversee and enforce the provisions of the 1974 Federal Election Campaign Act.
  c. scrutinize and attempt to discover loopholes in the 1974 Federal Election Campaign Act.
  d. oversee federal and state elections.
  e. limit soft money in campaigns.

5. Which of the following is a provision of the Bipartisan Campaign Reform Act of 2002?
  a. banning all soft-money contributions
  b. banning all outside special interest ads
  c. limiting individual contributions to $1,000 per individual
  d. banning only soft-money contribution to national political parties
  e. setting absolute campaign spending limits

6.   The Framers of the Constitution established the Electoral College because they wanted
     a.   to ensure the general population would have an opportunity to directly vote for president.
     b.   the choice of president and vice president to be made by a few dispassionate, reasonable men.
     c.   only candidates for president and vice president who had graduated from the Electoral College.
     d.   the political parties to be able to control the selection of president and vice president.
     e.   to increase the cost of campaigning so only the wealthy could be elected.

7.   The major parties are not in favor of eliminating the Electoral College because
     a.   the electors are always influential party members, and they might be offended.
     b.   the major party candidates would not receive as much public funding.
     c.   the masses are not capable of making this important decision.
     d.   they fear it would give minor parties a more influential role in the election outcome.
     e.   they fear it would lead to anarchy.

8.   The form of ballot that encourages straight-ticket voting is the
     a.   closed ballot.
     b.   open ballot.
     c.   office-block ballot.
     d.   party-column ballot.
     e.   electronic ballot.

9.   In the 2002 election, mail-in ballots were used extensively in the state of
     a.   California.
     b.   Texas.
     c.   New York
     d.   Arkansas.
     e.   Oregon.

10. Norman Ornstein criticizes mail-in voting because
     a.   it leads to massive fraud.
     b.   it will lead to Internet voting.
     c.   the mail is often late.
     d.   it will result in many uninformed votes.
     e.   it loses the sense of community needed for democracy.

11. Which provision of the Federal Election Campaign Act was declared unconstitutional in *Buckley v. Valeo*?
     a.   creation of the Federal Election Commission
     b.   limitations on campaign contributions
     c.   limitations on campaign spending
     d.   public financing of presidential elections
     e.   limiting of presidents to two terms

12. If we measure the influence of income on voting, then
     a.   the wealthy have the lowest turnout.
     b.   the poor have the lowest turnout.
     c.   as income rises, turnout declines.
     d.   the middle-income voter has the highest turnout.
     e.   there is no correlation between income and voting.

13. The rational ignorance effect refers to
     a.   the nomination of the presidential candidate.
     b.   campaign spending.
     c.   a reason why people vote.
     d.   a reason why people do not vote.
     e.   the voter registration process.

14. Which of the following measures to improve voter turnout have NOT been tried?
    a. mail-in voting
    b. registering when applying for a driver's license
    c. absentee voting
    d. an extended period of voting
    e. declaring Election Day a national holiday

15. Which of the following classes of people DO have the right to vote?
    a. noncitizens
    b. convicted felons
    c. election law violators
    d. current prison inmates
    e. disabled citizens

16. Since their introduction in the late nineteenth century, voter registration laws have
    a. increased the numbers of voters.
    b. reduced the voting of African Americans and immigrants.
    c. created a new class of active and committed voters.
    d. allowed for the manipulation of election results by party bosses.
    e. prevented fraud in elections.

17. When media sources transmit historical information, present American culture, and portray different regions and groups in the United States, these media are performing the role of
    a. providing entertainment.
    b. identifying public problems.
    c. socializing new generations.
    d. providing a political forum.
    e. making a profit.

18. Campaign staffers attempt to manage news coverage by
    a. trying to make the opposing candidate look bad.
    b. planning events that will be interesting enough to make the news.
    c. granting interviews and other forms of access to their candidate.
    d. both b and c
    e. all of the above

19. It has been suggested that the media have the greatest influence over
    a. voters who have picked their candidate already.
    b. voters who have not yet formed an opinion.
    c. those who always watch national news broadcasts.
    d. those who pay attention to polls.
    e. voters who see candidates on late-night talk shows.

20. To control and monitor what the public can access through the media, the government can do all of the following EXCEPT
    a. levy fines on broadcasters for indecency and profanity.
    b. restrict journalists' access to the military.
    c. censor blogs and websites.
    d. label government documents as "secret."
    e. The government cannot do any of these things.

Short Essay   Briefly address the major concepts raised by the following questions.

1. Describe the presidential election process from primaries to the general election.

2. Explain the legislative action taken to try to reform campaign financing.

3. Discuss the Electoral College procedures and proposed reforms.

4. List the six functions of mass media in America and explain how each can have a political impact.

ANSWERS TO THE PRACTICE EXAM

Fill-in-the-blank
1. recruited
2. white, male
3. political consultants
4. soft money
5. senators, representatives
6. office-block (or Massachusetts)
7. residency
8. *Buckley v. Valeo*
9. sound bite
10. Websites

True/False

1. F	3. F	5. T	7. T	9. F
2. T	4. T	6. F	8. F	10. T

Multiple Choice

1. c	5. d	9. e	13. d	17. c
2. d	6. b	10. d	14. e	18. d
3. b	7. d	11. c	15. e	19. b
4. b	8. d	12. b	16. b	20. c

Short Essay

1. Describe the presidential election process, from primaries to the general election.
The presidential process is comprised of two different campaigns, from January to November, linked together by the political party's national conventions.

- The presidential primary system begins with the Iowa caucus in January and the New Hampshire primary in February. The winner of these elections is dubbed the front-runner by the media, which gives that candidate a big boost in his/her campaign.
- States have moved their primary dates in recent years to boost their influence in the nomination of presidential candidates, a process which is known as front-loading. Southern states hold their primaries on the same date, known as Super Tuesday. Other states are now moving into January as well.
- The caucuses and primaries select delegates who go to the national convention. The main purpose of the national convention is to nominate the president and vice president.
- Around Labor Day, the president and vice president begin the campaign to capture the office in the general election held in November.

2. Explain the legislative action taken to try to reform campaign financing.
Congress, in 1925, passed a series of bills called the Corrupt Practices Acts, which were largely ineffective. The Hatch Act, passed in 1939, put limits on the amount of money that political groups could contribute to political campaigns.

The Federal Election Campaign Act of 1972 replaced the past laws and instituted a major reform.
After the Watergate scandal, the Federal Election Campaign Act reforms of 1974 were enacted. They did the following:

- created the Federal Election Commission
- provided public funding for presidential primaries and general elections
- limited presidential campaign spending
- limited contributions
- required disclosure

The decision of the Supreme Court in *Buckley v. Valeo* created a loophole that prompted the creation of Political Action Committees (PACs).
The Bipartisan Campaign Reform Act of 2002 prohibited soft money in federal elections.
Groups known as 527s have sprung up as a means of bypassing the most recent legislation.

3. Discuss the Electoral College procedures and proposed reforms.
The Electoral College is the constitutionally required method for the selection of the president and vice president.
Each state's electors are selected during the presidential election year. Each state is given the number of electors equal to that state's number of senators (two) plus its number of representatives.
The slate of electors in a state is elected by the candidate who has a plurality vote. In other words, the candidate who wins the most votes in that state wins all of the state's electoral votes. It takes 270 electoral votes to win the presidency.
The two major suggested reforms of the Electoral College are to abolish it entirely and elect the president by popular vote, or to require each elector by law to vote for the candidate that received the most popular votes.

4. List the six functions of mass media in America and explain how each can have a political impact.
Entertainment—dramatic television shows can introduce material that might be politically controversial.
Reporting the news—the media provide words and pictures about events, facts, and people and the free flow of information is important enough to the political process to be protected by the First Amendment.
Identifying public problems—the media can attract the attention of the public and of legislators to spur them to political action (such as the passage of laws that restrict the movements of sex offenders).
Socializing new generations—by portraying Americans and their habits and history, the media teach children and immigrants how to be "American."
Providing a political forum—this is a direct channel for political impact, as the media transmit political activities, debates, and commentary.
Making profits—this connection is less direct, but still influential. Media companies depend on advertising revenues to make money and these revenues are generally directly related to viewer/listener ratings. If a portion of the public does not like the political message a source puts forth, those viewers can stop watching or listening, driving ratings (and thus revenue) down. Also, if a specific advertiser objects to the political message of a broadcaster, that advertiser can pull its support or pressure the station to change. In both cases, "money talks."

Chapter 10
THE CONGRESS

CHAPTER SUMMARY

Congress is subject to a less-than-flattering national public opinion, but individual members of Congress are often seen favorably by the voters of their districts. Part of the explanation for this paradox is that while members of Congress spend their time serving their constituents, Congress as a whole was created to work for the nation. Understanding the nature of Congress is an important part of understanding the policy making that shapes life in America.

The Nature and Functions of Congress

The founders of the American republic thought that the bulk of government power should be in the hands of the legislative branch. The large versus small state division at the constitutional convention created a bicameral Congress, with one house—the House of Representatives—based on population and the other— the Senate—based on equality. The differences between the institutions in this bicameral Congress were further emphasized by term length: a two-year term for representatives in the House and a six-year term for senators. Congress has six basic functions: lawmaking, representation, service to constituents, oversight, public education, and conflict resolution. Lawmaking is an essential function of Congress, although the ideas for legislation frequently originate outside of Congress. Political tactics like compromise, logrolling, and debate are all employed to craft a majority coalition for a policy. Members of Congress can represent their constituency by acting as an instructed delegate, a tactic in which they vote according to the will of the people, or by acting as a trustee, a strategy in which legislators act according to their own conscience and the broad interests of the nation. Most legislators act in the politico style, combining the trustee and delegate styles of representation (reflecting the dual loyalties of Congresspersons to both their districts and the country as a whole). Service to constituents is vital to getting reelected and is accomplished by acting as the people's advocate—performing casework and acting as an ombudsperson for constituents who might be intimidated by governmental bureaucracy. The oversight function ensures that laws are being enforced and administered in the way Congress intended. The public education function has the important aspect of agenda setting, or determining what will come up for discussion and decision. The final function is to resolve conflicts in society by brokering compromises that satisfy differing (and often competing) ideologies or resource demands.

The Powers of Congress

The first seventeen clauses of Article I, Section 8 of the Constitution specify the enumerated powers of Congress. The most important domestic congressional powers are the powers to collect taxes, to spend, and to regulate commerce. The most important foreign policy power is the power to declare war. Some functions are restricted to the Senate, such as the approval of Supreme Court nominees. Constitutional amendments provide other powers to Congress. The final provision in Section 8 allows Congress to engage in actions that are necessary and proper to carry out the enumerated powers. The "necessary and proper," or "elastic," clause has allowed Congress to greatly expand its power and, in theory, it can act as a check against the expansion of executive power.

House-Senate Differences

Congress is composed of two very different but co-equal chambers. Size is the most marked difference: the House is much larger, at 435 members, while the Senate has 100 members (two from each state). A breakdown of the major differences between the House and Senate is presented in Table 10-1. The hefty size of the House of Representatives requires the Rules Committee to impose considerable procedural requirements and debate limits on the House, measures which can allow the House to act more quickly on legislation. The Senate allows unlimited debate, which can sometimes lead to the filibuster, a delaying tactic designed to block legislation. The Senate, with its smaller size and impressive slate of constitutional powers, is considered the more prestigious of the institutions.

Congresspersons and the Citizenry: A Comparison

Members of Congress are likely to be white, male, wealthy, and trained in a higher-status occupation, all of which are characteristics that set them apart from the U.S. population as a whole. (See Table 10-2 for a comparison of Congress and the U.S. population.) Although it remains an institution of the elite, Congress is more diverse in gender and ethnicity than ever before.

Congressional Elections

The process of electing members of Congress varies according to the election laws of each state. Many congressional candidates are self-recruited and have ties to the local district. As with presidential campaigns, the costs of congressional campaigns have greatly escalated. Congressional elections may be influenced in presidential election years by the coattail effect, but midterm elections frequently go against the congressional candidates from the president's party and the effect has failed to materialize at all in recent elections. (See Table 10-3 for midterm gains and losses from 1942 to 2006.) Incumbents enjoy enormous advantages and usually parlay those benefits into reelection. The incumbent can take advantage of name recognition, can claim credit for government programs that benefit constituents, and usually has more money than his or her challengers. (See Table 10-4 on the power of incumbency.) In spite of the advantage of incumbency, voters occasionally grow disenchanted with incumbents and replace them with challengers from the other party. This happened in the 2006 midterm elections when the Democrats took control of both houses of Congress from the Republicans, winning challenges and open seats alike.

Congressional Apportionment

After the census is conducted every ten years the seats in the House must be reallocated according to the latest population figures in a process called reapportionment. The state legislatures will redistrict or redraw the political boundaries to match the changes that have occurred in population. Legislatures have not always carried out this responsibility in a fair and acceptable manner. In a 1962 ruling, the Supreme Court stated that this matter could be reviewed by the court (was justiciable) and that the legislatures had to use the principle of "one person, one vote" to redistrict. Even though the issue of malapportionment is reviewable by the judiciary, the Supreme Court has been reluctant to become involved in these matters. In *Davis v. Bandemer* (1986), the Court agreed that heavy-handed redistricting could be challenged on constitutional grounds, but failed to come to an agreement on the unfairness of the districts in that specific case. Thus, gerrymandering continues, whether by packing supporters of the opposing party into as few districts as possible or by cracking those supporters into different districts to diffuse support. (See Figure 10-1 and Figure 10-2 for examples of different types of gerrymanders.) The federal government has encouraged some gerrymandering, such as the minority-majority districting in the 1990s meant to maximize the voting power of minority groups.

Perks and Privileges

Members of Congress receive a number of benefits that the average worker does not, including franking privileges. They are able to hire an extensive professional staff and use the resources and expertise of government agencies. Members of Congress are also exempt from certain laws that apply to the ordinary citizens, most notably from being sued for libel or slander. There are also a number of caucuses, which provide support for different subgroups of Congress. A rule prohibiting the use of public funds for caucuses was passed in 1995; now, caucuses are funded by businesses and special interest groups.

The Committee Structure

The committees and subcommittees of Congress perform most of the actual work of Congress. Committees are commonly known as "little legislatures" and they have control over their specific bills (control that is rarely taken from them through discharge petitions). There are several types of committees—standing, select, joint, and conference—as well as the specialized House Rules Committee. All of these committees have numerous subcommittees to whom work is delegated. Standing committees are permanent committees that are given a specific area of legislative expertise. (See Table 10-5 for a list of the standing committees of the 110th Congress.) Select committees are created for a limited time period and for a specific purpose. A joint committee is composed of members of both the House and Senate. A conference committee is a special joint committee created to achieve a compromise on different versions of the same bill. The House Rules Committee is unique to the House and is necessary to set rules for this large body. The Rules Committee defines the conditions under which legislation will be considered by the House. Members are appointed to standing committees by their party's Steering Committee and a system of seniority is used to select the chairpersons for the committees, though reforms in the 1970s and some appointments in 1995 shook seniority up slightly.

The Formal Leadership

The political parties organize the formal leadership of Congress. The leadership in the House is made up of the Speaker of the House, majority and minority leaders, and party whips. The Speaker of the House is the presiding officer of the House, a member of the majority party, and the most powerful member of the House. The majority leader is the leader of floor debate and cooperates with the Speaker. The minority leader is the leader of the minority party and speaks for the current president if the minority party controls the White House. Party officials called whips assist the leaders in Congress. The two most important formal leaders in the Senate are both ceremonial figures. The Constitution established the vice president as the presiding officer (president) of the Senate, but the vice president is rarely present for a meeting of the Senate. The Senate elects a president pro tempore ("pro tem") to preside in the absence of the vice president. The real leadership power in the Senate is held by the majority and minority floor leaders, who are assisted by whips. (See Table 10-6 for a complete list of the formal leadership structure in the 110th Congress.)

How Members of Congress Decide

It is difficult to establish all of the factors that determine how a member of Congress will vote. The single best predictor of how a member will vote seems to be political party membership. Party loyalty, however, is neither assured nor constant. How a member votes can also be influenced by cues from respected senior members and by regional and ideological differences or similarities among members and their districts.

How a Bill Becomes Law

The process of a bill becoming a law begins with the introduction of the bill in the House, the Senate, or both. A bill is referred to the appropriate committee and subcommittee, where the business of the legislative process occurs. The experts on the committee closely examine a bill. If the bill is approved and reported by the committee, it will be sent to the Rules Committee in the House or scheduled for floor debate in the Senate. The bill will be debated and voted on by the entire House and Senate. If a bill has passed the House and Senate in different forms, it will be sent to a conference committee so that a compromise can be hammered out. If that compromise is approved by both the House and Senate, the bill will be sent to the president for his signature or veto. (See Figure 10-3 for an illustration of this entire process.)

How Much Will the Government Spend?

The Constitution provides that all money bills must originate in the House of Representatives, yet the process usually begins with the executive branch. The president prepares and submits the executive budget to Congress for its approval. Budget conflicts with the president led Congress to pass the Budget and Impoundment Control Act in 1974. The federal government operates on a fiscal-year budget cycle that begins on October 1 of each year. The Office of Management and Budget (OMB) reviews each agency's budget request and prepares a budget, which the president submits to Congress in January. Congress then reviews the budget submitted by the president, ushers it through authorization and appropriation, and decides on the first budget resolution in May, which establishes the overall budget. The second budget resolution is supposed to be passed October 1 with the budget for each government agency. Often, Congress does not pass the second budget resolution by the deadline (thus breaking its own rules) in which case Congress must pass a continuing resolution to keep government agencies open until the new budget can be agreed upon. (See Figure 10-4 for an overview of the budget cycle.)

KEY TERMS

agenda setting	conference committee
appropriation	conservative coalition
authorization	constituent
bicameralism	continuing resolution
casework	direct primary

discharge petition
earmarks
enumerated power
executive budget
fall review
filibuster
first budget resolution
fiscal year (FY)
franking
gerrymandering
instructed delegate
joint committee
justiciable question
lawmaking
logrolling
majority leader of the House
minority leader of the House
ombudsperson

oversight
party identifier
president pro tempore
reapportionment
redistricting
representation
Rules Committee
safe seat
second budget resolution
select committee
Senate majority leader
Senate minority leader
seniority system
Speaker of the House
spring review
standing committee
Trustees
whip

OTHER RESOURCES

A number of valuable supplements are available to students using the Schmidt, Shelley, and Bardes text. A list of suggested supplements is at the end of the chapter. Ask your instructor how to obtain these resources. One supplement is highlighted here, www.senate.gov.

E-MOCRACY EXERCISES

Direct URL: http://www.senate.gov/general/contact_information/senators_cfm.cfm

Surfing Instructions:
Log on to www.senate.gov
Click on Senators in the upper left-hand corner.
From the drop down menu, select your state.
View one of your senators' Web pages by clicking on their name.

Study Questions
1. What kind of information is provided by your senator?
2. Do they provide information for contacting them? Is contacting them easily done?
3. Now select another senator and see how their Web page content differs.

PRACTICE EXAM
(Answers appear at the end of this chapter.)

Fill-in-the-Blank   Supply the missing word(s) or term(s) to complete the sentence.

1. America's founders believed that the bulk of the power that the national government would exercise should be in the hands of the _____.

2. According to the thinking of the Founders, the House was to be the _____ _____ chamber and the Senate was to be the chamber of the _____.

3. The division of a legislature into two separate assemblies is called _____.

4. The bulk of the bills that Congress acts upon come from the _____ _____.

5. _____ is the process by which Congress follows up on the laws it has enacted to ensure that they are being enforced and administered in the way Congress intended.

6. Under Senate Rule 22, debate may be ended by invoking _____, or shutting off discussion on a bill.

7. _____ are by far the largest occupational group among members of Congress.

8. The process of electing members of Congress is controlled by _____ _____.

9. The impact that a strong presidential candidate has on the ballot is called _____ _____ _____.

10. Committee chairpersons in Congress are usually selected by _____.

True/False   Circle the appropriate letter to indicate if the statement is true or false.

T   F   1. The Founding Fathers believed that the bulk of the power of the national government should be in the hands of the president.

T   F   2. The principle function of the legislature is lawmaking.

T   F   3. Instructed delegates mirror the views of the majority of their constituents.

T   F   4. The Rules Committee is the most powerful committee in the Senate.

T   F   5. Members of Congress must be cautious about what they say on the floor of Congress because of the possibility of being sued for slander.

T   F   6. The most important committees in Congress are the standing committees.

T   F   7. All money bills must originate in the House of Representatives.

T   F   8. Party membership is the single best predictor of how a member of Congress will vote on issues.

T   F   9. If Congress does not approve a budget by the beginning of the fiscal year, the government can continue to operate on continuing resolutions.

T   F   10. The most powerful individual in the House of Representatives is the Speaker of the House.

Multiple Choice   Circle the correct response.

1. The key characteristic of Congress as created by the Constitution was
    a. to have members directly elected by the people.
    b. a four-year term for all members.
    c. federalism.
    d. bicameralism.
    e. constituents.

2. The voting behavior of an instructed delegate would be to represent the
    a. majority view of his or her constituents.
    b. broad interests of society.
    c. interests of his or her party.
    d. president.
    e. most powerful interest groups.

3. The Senate is the chamber of the Congress that
   a. must first approve all money bills.
   b. must first approve amendments.
   c. ratifies treaties.
   d. has the first opportunity to override presidential vetoes.
   e. declares war.

4. Some functions are restricted to only one house of Congress. The Senate is the only house that can
   a. propose amendments.
   b. approve the budget.
   c. approve presidential appointments.
   d. investigate the president.
   e. originate revenue bills.

5. The central difference between the House and the Senate is that the
   a. House is much larger in membership than the Senate.
   b. House represents people while the Senate represents geography.
   c. House ratifies treaties.
   d. Senate first appropriates money.
   e. House can filibuster.

6. The largest occupational group among members of Congress is
   a. scientists.
   b. businesspersons.
   c. farmers.
   d. lawyers.
   e. educators.

7. In the House of Representatives,
   a. each state is allowed two representatives.
   b. no state can have more than twenty members.
   c. each state is allowed at least one representative.
   d. membership for each state is determined by the House itself.
   e. each state is allowed four representatives.

8. Most candidates for Congress must win the nomination for office in a
   a. party caucus.
   b. indirect primary.
   c. direct primary.
   d. party convention.
   e. nominating convention.

9. Midterm congressional elections in 1998 and 2002
   a. attracted as many voters as presidential elections.
   b. attracted more voters than presidential elections.
   c. resulted in the president's party losing seats in Congress.
   d. resulted in the president's party gaining seats in Congress.
   e. displayed no particular pattern.

10. The Supreme Court case of *Baker v. Carr* addressed the issue of
    a. foreign policy.
    b. budget policy.
    c. reapportionment.
    d. campaign spending.
    e. ethics in Congress.

11. The first seventeen clauses of Article I, Section 8 set forth the _____ powers of Congress.
    a. inherent
    b. implied
    c. enumerated
    d. stipulated
    e. necessitated

12. Gerrymandering refers to the process of
    a. ending debate in the Senate.
    b. redrawing legislative boundaries.
    c. forcing a bill out of committee.
    d. selecting a committee chair.
    e. eliminating debate in the House.

13. The phrase "little legislatures" refers to the
    a. legislatures that exist in the states.
    b. committees in Congress.
    c. departments of the federal bureaucracy.
    d. interest groups that lobby Congress.
    e. states with few electoral votes.

14. The "third house of Congress" refers to
    a. standing committees.
    b. select committees.
    c. special committees.
    d. conference committees.
    e. the media.

15. In the House of Representatives, the majority leader
    a. acts as spokesperson for the majority party in the House.
    b. serves as Speaker of the House.
    c. is elected in a vote of all the members of the House.
    d. is rarely able to exert any meaningful leadership because of the dominance of the Speaker.
    e. is just a ceremonial figure.

16. The congressional budget process was very disjointed until the passage of the
    a. Office of Management and Budget.
    b. Budget and Impoundment Control Act.
    c. Discharge Petition.
    d. Council of Economic Advisers.
    e. Budget Director Act.

17. The fiscal year (FY) of the federal government extends from
    a. January to December.
    b. April to February.
    c. October to September.
    d. July to June.
    e. December to January.

18. The federal agency that prepares the budget is the
    a. Economic Agency.
    b. Office of Management and Budget.
    c. Congress.
    d. Council of Economic Advisers.
    e. Appropriations Committee.

19. A continuing resolution allows
    a. congresspersons to remain in office after their term.
    b. a nearly passed law to remain in the new session of Congress.
    c. government agencies to continue to function if a new budget is not passed.
    d. the president to set the budget without Congress.
    e. a law to take effect immediately.

20. One of the most important decisions for Congress that affects our lives every day is
    a. whether minority groups are protected.
    b. how much the government spends.
    c. reforming the Electoral College.
    d. figuring out how to provide direction for all of the young people elected to Congress.
    e. how to reform Social Security.

Short Essay   Briefly address the major concepts raised by the following questions:

1. Explain the major functions of Congress.

2. Describe the formal leadership positions in the House of Representatives and the Senate.

3. Discuss the steps that a bill goes through to become law.

ANSWERS TO THE PRACTICE EXAM

Fill-in-the-blank
1. legislature
2. common man's, elite
3. bicameralism
4. executive branch
5. Oversight
6. cloture
7. Lawyers
8. state legislatures
9. the coattail effect
10. seniority

True/False

1. F	3. T	5. F	7. T	9. T
2. T	4. F	6. T	8. T	10. T

Multiple Choice

1. d	6. d	11. c	16. b
2. a	7. c	12. b	17. c
3. c	8. c	13. b	18. b
4. c	9. d	14. d	19. c
5. a	10. c	15. a	20. b

Short Essay

1. Explain the major functions of Congress.

There are six major functions of Congress: lawmaking, service to constituents, representation, oversight, public education, and conflict resolution.
   • Lawmaking is the principal and most obvious function of a legislative body.

- Service to constituents is primarily carried out by doing casework and by acting as an ombudsperson with government agencies.
- Members of Congress can represent constituents by being a trustee or instructed delegate.
- The oversight function is for Congress to follow up on laws enacted, to see that they are being enforced and administered as intended.
- The public education function of Congress is to assist in agenda setting.
- Conflict resolution is a key function for government to resolve issues of scarce resources and differences in societal goals.

2.   Describe the formal leadership positions in the House of Representatives and the Senate.

(See Table 10-6 for a complete list of the current individuals who hold leadership positions.)
Leadership in the House consists of the Speaker, the majority and minority leaders, and party whips.
- The Speaker is the most important leader in the House, who presides, makes appointments, schedules legislation, decides points of order, and refers bills.
- The majority and minority leaders are elected in party caucus and act as spokespersons and leaders of their party.
- Whips are assistants to the party leaders.

Leadership in the Senate consists of the U.S. vice president, president pro tempore, majority and minority leaders, and party whips.
- The Constitution creates the President of the Senate, the vice president, as the ceremonial leader of the Senate.
- The Senate elects another ceremonial leader, president pro tempore, to preside over the Senate in the vice president's absence.
- The real leadership power in the Senate rests with the majority and minority leaders.
- Whips are assistants to Senate party leaders.

3.   Discuss the steps that a bill goes through to become law.

(See Figure 10-3 for an illustration of the entire legislative process.)
The bill is introduced to the House or Senate or both.
The bill is referred to the appropriate committee.
The bill is referred to subcommittee.
The full committee reports on the bill.
The Rules Committee in the House establishes rules for the bill.
The entire House debates the bill and votes on it.
The same steps, except for the Rules Committee, occur in the Senate.
Conference action may be required to clear up differences between the House and Senate.
The bill goes to the president for approval or veto.

Chapter 11
THE PRESIDENT

CHAPTER SUMMARY

Who Can Become President?

The constitutional requirements for becoming president are that a person must be a natural born citizen, at least 35 years old, and a resident of the United States for at least 14 years. The informal "requirements," gleaned from the list of past presidents, suggest the president is likely to be an older, white, Protestant male.

The Process of Becoming President

The voters of the general public do not directly vote for president and vice president; instead, their votes are cast for electors, who compose the Electoral College and cast the official vote for president. On a few occasions, the Electoral College has failed to elect a president, and the House of Representatives was compelled to break the tie. The Twelfth Amendment, adopted in 1804, clarified one aspect of this process by separating the Electoral College election of the president and vice president.

The Many Roles of the President

The Constitution established the following five major roles for the president: head of state, chief executive, commander-in-chief of the armed forces, chief diplomat, and chief legislator of the United States. The head of state role is dismissed by some as simply symbolic, but in times of crisis or celebration (such as the Great Depression or decoration of war heroes), the head of state role can provide support and guidance or symbolize the "dignity and majesty" of the American people. The chief executive function requires the president, as the head of the executive branch, to see that the laws are "faithfully execute[d]"; this loose wording is a source of constitutional power for the executive. The federal bureaucracy (with its 2.7 million employees) assists the president in carrying out executive responsibilities. The president also has appointive power to fill some of the most important positions in government. (See Table 11-1 for a list of these positions.) Lastly, under executive power, the president can grant reprieves and pardons for all federal crimes (except in cases of impeachment). As commander-in-chief of the armed forces, the president represents civilian control of the military. Presidents have probably exercised more authority in this role than in any other. Not all presidents have exercised this power in a prudent fashion, which led Congress in 1973 to attempt to gain more control over military actions with the War Powers Resolution. In spite of this resolution, the powers of the president as commander-in-chief are still extensive. Under the role of chief diplomat, the president is given the power to recognize foreign governments, to make treaties with the approval of the Senate, and to conduct general United States foreign policy. Presidents have greatly expanded their power in foreign policy through the use of executive agreements, which, unlike treaties, do not require Senate approval. The president's position of chief legislator is, constitutionally, the requirement that the president present legislation to Congress; in modern times, the president has played a large role in determining what Congress will address through the annual State of the Union message. In addition, as chief legislator the president works to ensure that his or her programs are enacted into law by Congress. Another aspect of the president's role as chief legislator is the power the office possesses to veto legislation passed by Congress. The president's veto power was created as an "all or nothing" proposition, in which he or she is forced to make a decision between accepting an entire piece of legislation and signing it into law or vetoing the legislation in its entirety. In the 1990s, Congress expanded the veto to allow the president to veto specific line-items in spending bills without rejecting the entire bill, but the Supreme Court ruled this expansion of presidential power to be unconstitutional. (See Table 11-2 for past presidents' use of the veto.) Presidents sometimes utilize a signing statement when signing a bill into law. These statements are increasingly common and they often address parts of the law that the president believes may be either unconstitutional or may be contrary to the national security interests of the country. The constitutional legality of such statements has yet to be challenged in court. Finally, the president also possesses powers that are inherent in the office of the president as well as those powers that are given to the office by statutes enacted by Congress.

The President as Party Chief and Superpolitician

Although the Constitution mentions nothing about party leadership, the president does function as head of his or her political party. Historically, a major tool of the president as party leader was patronage, which was more extensive in the past but still has some influence today. As presidents lead their parties, they must consider three different constituencies: the general public (including nonvoters), the members of the political parties, and the Washington community. How successful the president is with these constituencies is measured by the presidential approval rating. George W. Bush presents a veritable case study in the significance, and the inconsistency, of public opinion. While his public approval ratings after September 11, 2001 were the highest ever recorded, by the time he ran for reelection they had dipped to approximately fifty percent and in his second term they have plummeted to thirty four percent. (See Figure 11-1 for a look at the approval ratings of modern presidents.) Presidents have also used the strategy of "going public" to persuade and manipulate public opinion outside the facilities of government.

Special Uses of Presidential Power

There are a number of powers and privileges available only to the president. The president is able to employ emergency powers to respond to situations of crisis, as was demonstrated by Abraham Lincoln in the Civil War and Franklin Roosevelt during World War II. The Supreme Court recognized these powers in *United States v. Curtiss-Wright Export Corporation* (1936). The president also has the power to issue executive orders, which have the force of law and must be published in the *Federal Register*. In recent years executive orders have been used to classify secret government information, to establish military tribunals for suspected terrorists and to establish the Peace Corps. Finally, the president possesses the power of executive privilege, or the ability of the president and other executive officials to withhold information from legislative committees. In *United States v. Nixon* (1974), the Supreme Court acknowledged the legitimacy of executive privilege, but found that Nixon's argument that executive privilege justified the withholding of tapes of White House conversations from Congress and the courts was illegitimate. Bill Clinton was also unsuccessful in his invocation of executive privilege during the investigation of his relationship with Monica Lewinsky. More recently, President Bush has claimed executive privilege in multiple cases. He refused Congress' request to have Tom Ridge, the head of the Department of Homeland Security, and other top White House aids testify about Executive Department misconduct. Bush also refused to allow the Government Accountability Office to obtain documents regarding Vice President Dick Cheney's energy policy task force.

Abuses of Executive Power and Impeachment

The Constitution empowers the House and Senate to remove the president, vice president, or other civil officials for treason, bribery, and other high crimes and misdemeanors. The House first impeaches the officer and the Senate then conducts the trial. Although two presidents have been impeached, no president has been convicted and thus removed from office. Andrew Johnson was impeached in 1868 for his failure to faithfully execute laws that he believed were unconstitutional. Richard Nixon was about to be impeached for obstruction of justice and violation of the Constitution in 1974, but he resigned before the vote was held. Lastly, Bill Clinton was impeached in 1998 for obstruction of justice and perjury.

The Executive Organization

At the beginning of Franklin Roosevelt's tenure as president, the number of presidential staff totaled thirty-seven; today the staff is over six hundred people. The president's cabinet began with four officials; today there are fifteen department secretaries and the attorney general. Modern presidents do not use the cabinet as a true advisory group but prefer to rely on informal advisers, sometimes called the kitchen cabinet. In 1939, President Franklin Roosevelt issued an executive order creating the Executive Office of the President (EOP) to provide staff assistance to the president. The EOP consists of many staff agencies, ranging from offices of science or drug control to councils on the economy or environment. One of the most important agencies in the EOP is the White House Office, which includes most of the key personnel and advisers to the president. In recent presidencies, the chief of staff has been in charge of coordinating the White House Office. In 1970, President Nixon reorganized the previous Bureau of the Budget to create the Office of Management and Budget (OMB), which prepares the federal budget and advises the president on management techniques. The president's assistant for national security affairs brings together the president's foreign policy and military advisers.

The Vice Presidency

The Constitution gives the vice president very little power; his or her only formal job is to preside over the Senate and to vote in case of a tie. Traditionally, candidates for vice president have been selected for political reasons, like strengthening or balancing a ticket, rather than based on a careful consideration of whether they would make good presidents. But eight times in U.S. history the vice president has ascended to the highest office in the land through the death of the president. Article II, Section 1 of the Constitution stipulates that the vice president receives the powers of the president in the case of incapacitation or death, but not until 1967—notably after all eight successions—was a mechanism provided for filling presidential and vice presidential vacancies with the Twenty-Fifth Amendment, which also addresses situations in which the president is incapable of discharging the duties of the office. For the selection of a new vice president, Congress advises on and consents to a candidate selected by the president. This process was first put to use with the resignation of Richard Nixon's vice president, Spiro Agnew, when Congress confirmed Gerald Ford as the new vice president. Then when President Nixon resigned the next year, Ford (now the first completely un-voted-on president) selected Nelson Rockefeller for his vice president. (See Table 11-3 for the full line of succession to the presidency.)

KEY TERMS

advice and consent
appointment power
cabinet
chief diplomat
chief executive
chief legislator
chief of staff
civil service
commander-in-chief
constitutional power
diplomatic recognition
emergency power
executive agreement
Executive Office of the President (EOP)
executive privilege
expressed power
Federal Register
head of state
impeachment

inherent power
kitchen cabinet
line-item veto
National Security Council (NSC)
Office of Management and Budget OMB)
pardon
patronage
pocket veto
reprieve
signing statement
State of the Union message
statutory power
Twelfth Amendment
Twenty-Fifth Amendment
veto message
War Powers Resolution
Washington community
White House Office

OTHER RESOURCES

A number of valuable supplements are available to students using the Schmidt, Shelley, and Bardes text. A list of suggested supplements is at the end of the chapter. Ask your instructor how to obtain these resources. One supplement is highlighted here, the White House's Web site.

E-MOCRACY EXERCISES

Direct URL: http://www.whitehouse.gov/radio/

Surfing Instructions:
Log on to www.whitehouse.gov
On the left hand side of the screen, locate the "News" heading.
Click on "Radio."

Select the most recent Presidential Radio Address from the center of the page. You can either read the text by clicking on the date of the address or listen to the most recent by clicking "play audio."

Study Questions

1. The tradition of a presidential radio address dates back to President Franklin Roosevelt and his 1930s fireside chats. Do you believe that this is still an effective or relevant medium for the President to disseminate his weekly message?
2. Did the President adequately and clearly explain the issues facing the country this week?
3. This address is one of the only unfiltered ways in which the President can get his message out to the country without a reporter's interpretation. Do you believe that the context and background provided by a reporter's interpretation would help or hinder your understanding of this message?

PRACTICE EXAM
(Answers appear at the end of this chapter.)

Fill-in-the-Blank   Supply the missing word(s) or term(s) to complete the sentence.

1. The _____ Amendment clarified aspects of Electoral College voting.

2. The president decorating war heroes is an example of the presidential role as _____ ___ _____.

3. The president is constitutionally bound to enforce the acts of Congress, the judgments of federal courts, and treaties in the role of _____ _____.

4. The constitution gives the president the power to grant _____ and _____ for offenses against the United States except in cases of impeachment.

5. Presidential power in foreign affairs is greatly enhanced by the use of _____ _____ made between the president and other heads of state.

6. Powers given to the president by law are called _____ _____.

7. The formal indictment of the president for wrongdoing by the House of Representatives is called _____.

8. The presidential advisory group composed of the secretaries of the executive departments is called the _____.

9. The official responsible for coordinating the White House Office is the _____ _____ _____.

10. The only formal duty of the vice president found in the Constitution is to preside over the _____.

True/False   Circle the appropriate letter to indicate if the statement is true or false.

T   F   1.   A presidential candidate cannot win the Electoral College vote without getting a majority of the popular vote.

T   F   2.   In most democratic governments, the role of head of state is given to someone other than the chief executive.

T   F   3.   The president's extensive appointment powers allow him to control and run the federal bureaucracy to suit his or her desires.

T   F   4.   The president may grant reprieves and pardons for all offenses against the United States except in cases of contempt of court.

T   F   5.   The president has the sole power to recognize or refuse to recognize foreign governments.

T   F   6. Executive agreements made by the president and the heads of other governments must be ratified by the Senate.

T   F   7. The presidential veto is an effective legislative tool because Congress rarely can override it.

T   F   8. Emergency powers are the most common example of inherent powers exercised by the president.

T   F   9. An executive order has the force of law.

T   F   10. Most presidents have relied heavily on their cabinet members for advice in decision making.

Multiple Choice   Circle the correct response.

1. The most common occupation of presidents has been that of
   a. teacher.
   b. lawyer.
   c. businessman.
   d. farmer.
   e. doctor.

2. In the event that no candidate receives a majority of the Electoral College votes, the president is selected by the
   a. Senate from the two candidates receiving the most electoral votes.
   b. Senate from any candidates receiving electoral votes.
   c. Congress from any person they choose to elect.
   d. House of Representatives, choosing from the three candidates receiving the most electoral votes.
   e. Supreme Court.

3. The activity most typical of the head of state role is
   a. developing military strategy.
   b. offering the State of the Union message.
   c. negotiating treaties with foreign governments.
   d. receiving visiting heads of state at the White House.
   e. granting a pardon.

4. The president can remove all of the following from office except
   a. federal judges.
   b. the heads of cabinet departments.
   c. individuals within the Executive Office of the President.
   d. the director of the E.P.A.
   e. political appointees.

5. The effect of the constitutional requirement that the president "shall be the Commander in Chief of the Army and Navy" is to
   a. require the president to be a commissioned officer.
   b. distort the lines of authority within the command structure of the armed forces.
   c. require the president to take instruction at one of the service academies.
   d. place the armed forces under civilian, rather than military, control.
   e. cause conflicts with the secretary of defense.

6. The role in which the president has probably exercised more authority than in any other role is
   a. chief administrator.
   b. chief of the party.

  c. commander-in-chief.
  d. chief legislator.
  e. chief diplomat.

7. The activity typical of the role of chief diplomat is
    a. vetoing foreign policy legislation.
    b. delivering the State of the Union message.
    c. meeting with state governors to discuss federal aid.
    d. declaring war.
    e. negotiating treaties with foreign governments.

8. A typical activity associated with the role of chief legislator is
    a. recognizing representatives from foreign governments.
    b. negotiating treaties with foreign governments.
    c. meeting with state party leaders to discuss campaign strategy.
    d. offering the annual State of the Union message.
    e. decorating war heroes.

9. The only requirement of a president when issuing an executive order is that the executive order must
    a. pertain to legislatively authorized items.
    b. deal with only military matters.
    c. deal only with the Executive Office of the President.
    d. be designated as an emergency by Congress.
    e. be published in the *Federal Register*.

10. Executive privilege
    a. means that no member of the executive branch can be prosecuted for any act while they are performing their job.
    b. is the concept that has been applied to the president's use of a pocket veto during a session of Congress.
    c. protects the president and the cabinet from impeachment proceedings.
    d. involves the ability of the president to withhold certain information from Congress and/or the courts.
    e. has been ruled unconstitutional by the Supreme Court.

11. The last president impeached by the House of Representatives was
    a. Lyndon Johnson.
    b. Andrew Johnson.
    c. Richard Nixon.
    d. Bill Clinton.
    e. George W. Bush.

12. The agency that includes most of the key personal and political advisers to the president is in the
    a. cabinet.
    b. Congress.
    c. White House Office.
    d. National Security Council.
    e. Office of Management and Budget.

13. Which statement is **correct** about the vice president's job?
    a. The Constitution gives several important powers to the vice president.
    b. The Constitution makes the vice president the number one advisor to the president.
    c. Earlier vice presidents had more to do than our recent vice presidents have.
    d. The vice president is in charge of emergency situations.
    e. The Constitution does not give much power to the vice president.

14. The constitutional amendment establishing procedures for presidential succession and disability is the
    a. Twelfth Amendment.
    b. Twenty-Fourth Amendment.
    c. Twenty-Fifth Amendment.
    d. Twenty-Seventh Amendment.
    e. Twenty-Eighth Amendment.

15. The question of who shall be president if both the president and vice president die is answered by
    a. the Twenty-Fifth Amendment.
    b. a special election to fill the vacancy.
    c. the Succession Act of 1947.
    d. the Twelfth Amendment.
    e. the Twenty-Seventh Amendment.

16. The only president to use the line-item veto was
    a. Ronald Reagan.
    b. George H. W. Bush.
    c. Bill Clinton.
    d. Richard Nixon.
    e. George W. Bush.

17. The constituency that measures presidential performance and power on a daily basis is the
    a. party constituency.
    b. Congress.
    c. Washington community.
    d. media in rural areas.
    e. Internet.

18. The style of presidential leadership has changed since World War II because of
    a. stronger political parties.
    b. constitutional amendments.
    c. the influence of the League of Nations.
    d. post-modernity.
    e. the influence of television and the increase of presidents "going public" with their messages.

19. The emergency powers of the president were recognized in
    a. *U.S. v. Curtiss-Wright Export Corp.*
    b. *Youngstown Steel and Tube Co. v. Sawyer.*
    c. *U.S. v. Nixon.*
    d. *Train v. City of New York.*
    e. the *Federal Register.*

20. Which of the following is **not** in the Executive Office of the President?
    a. White House Office staff
    b. Office of the Vice President
    c. Council of Economic Advisers
    d. Office of Management and Budget
    e. Attorney General

Short Essay   Briefly address the major concepts raised by the following questions.

1. Identify and explain the roles of the president.

2. Trace the development of the sources of presidential power.

3. Describe the organization of the executive branch and how it has evolved over time.

4. Discuss the evolving role for the vice president as an advisor and successor to the president.

ANSWERS TO THE PRACTICE EXAM

Fill-in-the-Blank
1. Twelfth
2. head of state
3. chief executive
4. reprieves, pardons
5. executive agreements
6. statutory powers
7. impeachment
8. cabinet
9. chief of staff
10. Senate

True/False

1. F	3. F	5. T	7. T	9. T
2. T	4. F	6. F	8. T	10. F

Multiple Choice

1. b	5. d	9. e	13. e	17. c
2. d	6. c	10. d	14. c	18. e
3. d	7. e	11. d	15. c	19. a
4. a	8. d	12. c	16. c	20. e

Short Essay

1.   Identify and explain the roles of the president.
There are five constitutional roles of the president: 1) head of state, 2) chief executive, 3) commander-in-chief, 4) chief diplomat, and 5) chief legislator.
The head of state role consists of ceremonial functions (such as decorating war heroes), hosting chiefs of state, telephoning sports and space heroes, and dedicating parks.
The chief executive role is to see that the laws are carried out. The president makes appointments of key individuals to carry out this function. He can also grant reprieves or pardons under executive authority.
Commander-in-chief is probably the president's most powerful role. It embodies the principle of civilian control of the military.
The chief diplomat role involves the making of treaties with the consent of the Senate and recognizing foreign governments as legitimate.
The chief legislator role includes the delivery of the State of the Union message every year and the use of veto power in relationship to laws passed by Congress.

2.   Trace the development of the sources of presidential power.
There are four major sources of presidential power: 1) the Constitution, 2) statutes, 3) expressed power, and 4) inherent power.

Constitutional powers of the president are contained in Article II, and are the powers (roles) discussed in essay one.

Statutory power is created for the president through laws enacted by Congress, such the power to declare national emergencies.

Expressed powers are those that are specifically written into the Constitution or laws.

Inherent powers are those that can be inferred from loosely worded constitutional statements, such as "the executive power shall be vested in a President." Emergency powers invoked by the president during wartime are good examples of inherent powers.

3. Describe the organization of the executive branch and how it has evolved over time.

The administration of George Washington developed an advisory group, the cabinet, composed of the heads of the executive departments.

Beginning with President Andrew Jackson, presidents used an informal group of advisors referred to as the kitchen cabinet.

President Franklin Roosevelt greatly expanded the administrative staff of the president through the creation of the Executive Office of the President (EOP) in 1939. The key parts of the EOP are:

- the White House Office, which is coordinated by the chief of staff and provides the president with whatever he needs to carry out presidential duties.
- the Council of Economic Advisers (CEA), which advises the president on economic policy.
- the Office of Management and Budget (OMB), which prepares the budget and advises the president on management and planning.
- the National Security Council, which advises the president on military and security issues.

4. Discuss the evolving role of the vice president as an advisor and successor to the president.

The only role for the vice president mentioned in the Constitution is to preside over the Senate.

Vice presidents have traditionally been selected to balance the ticket.

Eight vice presidents have become presidents because of the death of the president.

The Constitution provided no process to select a new vice president.

The Twenty-Fifth Amendment provides for a process to select a new vice president and in case of presidential disability.

The Succession Act of 1947 provides for the situation in which both the president and vice president die.

Chapter 12
THE BUREAUCRACY

CHAPTER SUMMARY

Politics in America is marked by a contradiction: the majority of Americans say they would prefer "less government," but at the same time, they also report that they support almost all of the programs of the national bureaucracy—programs that can only be supplied by a large organization.

The Nature of Bureaucracy

The national government, with its size, structure, and specific functions, represents a very visible bureaucracy. Bureaucracy can exist in both the public and private sectors, but unlike corporate organizations, public bureaucracies do not have a single set of leaders, are not organized to make a profit, and are not necessarily efficient or responsive to change. (See Table 12-1 for presidential efforts to end government inefficiency.) There are several different theories about how bureaucracies function. The Weberian model views bureaucracies as rational, hierarchical organizations in which power flows from the top down. The acquisitive model focuses on the belief that top-level bureaucrats always try to expand their budgets and staffs. The monopolistic model proposes that bureaucracies are like business monopolies; due to a similar lack of competition, they are therefore likely to be less efficient and more costly to operate. The federal bureaucracy in the United States enjoys a greater degree of autonomy than do those of other countries in part because its lines of authority are not well defined. In the U.S., the federal nature of government means that national bureaucracies often give financial support to their counterparts at the state level. Additionally, the U.S. government bureaucracy does not own and operate utilities; it does, however, have a hand in regulation through a handful of administrative agencies.

The Size of the Bureaucracy

The federal bureaucracy began in 1789 with three departments—State, War, and Treasury—and a handful of employees. Today, the fifteen executive departments of government and other agencies employ approximately 2.7 million employees. (See Figure 12-1 for a look at the government civilian employees by agency and Figure 12-2 for employees at the various levels of government.)

The Organization of the Federal Bureaucracy

The federal bureaucracy has four major types of structures: cabinet departments, independent executive agencies, independent regulatory agencies, and government corporations. (See Figure 12-3 for an organizational chart of the federal government.) The fifteen cabinet (executive) departments, which can be described as line organizations, are the major part of the federal bureaucracy. (See Table 12-2.) Independent executive agencies are bureaucratic organizations that are not part of a department but still report directly to the president. (See Table 12-3 for a brief description of various independent executive agencies.) Independent regulatory agencies are responsible for regulating a particular sector of the economy for the public interest. With this purpose, each agency acts as its own executive, legislative, and judicial branch. Due to corporate involvement (and the re- and deregulation of some sectors), some claim these regulatory agencies are not truly independent, having been captured by their industries. (See Table 12-4 for information on selected independent regulatory agencies.) Government corporations are agencies that administer a quasi-business enterprise. The U.S. Postal Service is a good example of this type of bureaucratic entity. (See Table 12-5 for information on selected government corporations.)

Staffing the Bureaucracy

There are two categories of a bureaucrat: political appointees and civil servants. Political appointees are selected to the top positions in the government by the president. The average term of a political appointee is two years. The career civil servants, who make up the bulk of the bureaucracy, can thus afford to wait out political appointees that they do not agree with. In 1789, the first federal government employed no career public servants, but rather a group of Federalist amateurs. Thomas Jefferson oversaw the mass firing of more than 100 officials, replacing them with officials of his own party. When Andrew Jackson became president, he resoundingly implemented the spoils system, packing federal positions with his supporters. In 1883, the Civil Service Reform Act (also known as the Pendleton Act) brought about substantial reform by replacing the spoils system with a merit system and creating the Civil Service Commission to administer the personnel service. The Civil Service Commission was abolished by the Civil Service Reform Act of 1978, which created the Office of Personnel Management (OPM) to improve the quality of individuals hired by agencies and the Merit Systems Protection Board (MSPB) to regulate the relations between agencies and employees. In 1939, the Hatch Act was passed to protect government workers from political manipulation. The reach of the Hatch Act has been debated, with many saying it violates the First Amendment and others contending that it is necessary to preserve a nonpartisan civil service.

Modern Attempts at Bureaucratic Reform

The government continues to attempt reforms of the bureaucracy and make it more responsive to the needs of U.S. citizens. In 1976, Congress passed the Government in the Sunshine Act. This law required all committee-directed agencies to conduct their business regularly in public session. The reaction to 9/11 has been to allow fewer agencies to operate "in the sunshine," based on the fear that our enemies would be able to access certain information that could be used to plan terrorist attacks. Sunset legislation is designed to review existing programs regularly for their effectiveness and to terminate programs unless the review establishes that they should be continued. Unfortunately, this idea has never been adopted by Congress, but most states utilize it. Another approach to bureaucratic reform is to contract out services to the private sector, with an eye toward producing greater efficiency. In recent years the extensive use of private contractors for defense department war efforts has come under great scrutiny. Criticisms range from a lack of competitive bidding, oversight and accountability. Other incentives for efficiency and productivity are also used to influence the bureaucracy for the better. The Government Performance and Results Act of 1997 was designed to improve efficiency in the federal work force; agencies were to set goals and establish a means of measuring whether the goals were reached. Finally, several protections have been put in place for whistleblowers who report bureaucratic waste and inappropriate behavior. The Civil Service Reform Act of 1978 set up the Merit Systems Protection Board and in 1989, Congress passed the Whistleblower Protection Act, which established the Office of the Special Counsel. Both acts intended to facilitate internal regulation of government agencies by their employees. In 2006, the Supreme Court's decision in *Garcetti v. Ceballos* reversed this protectionist trend by supporting the punishment of an assistant district attorney for attempting to expose a lie. Congress is currently considering legislation to further extend whistleblower protections to civil servants at national security agencies, employees of government contractors, and federal workers who expose the distortion of scientific data for political purpose.

Bureaucrats as Politicians and Policymakers

Congress is unable to oversee the day-to-day administration of its programs, so it delegates this authority to administrative agencies through what is called enabling legislation. Agencies are empowered to make rules and regulations that carry out the will of Congress. The agencies hold public hearings about the matters to be covered by rules and all new regulations must be published in the *Federal Register*. Groups subject to regulation can engage in a process called negotiated rulemaking, which allows these groups to participate in the drafting of the rules with the caveat that the groups then cannot challenge the outcome of their agreements in court. Traditional theories of bureaucracy once assumed that bureaucrats do not make policy decisions, but merely enforce the policy decisions made by the people's elected representatives. The reality is that bureaucrats have the opportunity to shape policy, as is illustrated by the presence of iron triangles and issue networks, in which bureaucrats interact with other major players in our system to produce policy decisions. Agencies can also affect policy by either refusing to implement a particular law or by over-zealous enforcement. The EPA, under pressure from Congress and the president, refused to regulate carbon dioxide and other greenhouse gasses. Ultimately the Supreme Court forced the agency to do so.

Congressional Control of the Bureaucracy

Although Congress cannot oversee the day-to-day operations of the bureaucracy, it can, theoretically, still control the bureaucracy through authorization and appropriation of funds and by investigation and oversight hearings. Two agencies it can put into service are the Government Accountability Office and the Congressional Budget Office. However, Congress' investigation and control will not expose all of the problems involved in the bureaucracy; both its "police patrol" and "fire alarm" approaches will fail to detect some problems. The Bush administration implemented an executive order aimed at further controlling the branch's agencies. Each federal agency is required to establish an Regulatory Policy Officer whose job it is to bring agency rulemaking and interpretation into line with the policies of the current administration. This controversial order can be interpreted as both an attempt to streamline agencies and a great potential for the further politicization of policy implementation.

KEY TERMS

acquisitive model
administrative agency
bureaucracy
cabinet department
capture
Civil Service Commission
enabling legislation
government corporation
Government in the Sunshine Act
independent executive agency
independent regulatory agency

iron triangle
issue network
line organization
merit system
monopolistic model
Pendleton Act (Civil Service Reform Act)
Privatization
spoils system
sunset legislation
Weberian model
whistleblower

OTHER RESOURCES

A number of valuable supplements are available to students using the Schmidt, Shelley, and Bardes text. A list of suggested supplements is at the end of the chapter. Ask your instructor how to obtain these resources. One supplement is highlighted here, the *Federal Register*.

E-MOCRACY EXERCISES

Direct URL: http://www.gpoaccess.gov/usbudget/fy08/browse.html

Surfing Instructions:
Log on to www.gpoaccess.gov/fr/index.html
At the top of the page, click on "Executive."
Under Presidential Materials, click on the link for the "Budget of the United States Government."
Click on Browse the FY09 Budget (FY09 stands for Fiscal Year 2009. Select the current year applicable.)
Select one of the sections of the federal budget and view its PDF.

Study Questions
1. After reading a section, do you believe that this document has provided a good understanding about where our tax dollars are being spent?
2. Does the document provide enough detail or is it general in description?
3. Are there any political aspects to the wording used?

PRACTICE EXAM
(Answers appear at the end of this chapter.)

Fill-in-the-Blank   Supply the missing word(s) or term(s) to complete the sentence.

1. A _____ is the name given to a large organization that is structured hierarchically and is supposed to carry out specific functions.

2. The classic model of the modern bureaucracy is the _____ model.

3. The major service organizations of the federal government are the fifteen _____ _____.

4. _____ _____ _____ are bureaucratic organizations that are not located within a department and report directly to the president.

5. The earliest independent regulatory agency created was the _____ _____ _____.

6. The form of bureaucratic organization borrowed from business is the _____ _____.

7. The president generally associated with the spoils system is _____ _____.

8. Replacing government services with services from the private sector is called _____.

9. The three-way alliance among legislators, bureaucrats, and interest groups to benefit their respective interests is called the _____ _____.

10. The law that specifies the name, purpose, functions, and powers of an agency is _____ _____.

True/False   Circle the appropriate letter to indicate if the statement is true or false.

T   F   1. Modern presidents have been able to exert power over the bureaucracy in order to shape it to their own desires.

T   F   2. The federal bureaucracy in the United States is much more controlled and restricted than are the bureaucracies of other countries.

T   F   3. Cabinet departments can be described in management terms as line organizations.

T   F   4. Regulatory agencies are independent because they are administered independently of all three branches of government.

T   F   5. The assassination of President James Garfield had an impact on civil service reform.

T   F   6. The Hatch Act prohibits federal civil service employees from engaging in political campaigns.

T   F   7. Today, few states have sunset laws.

T   F   8. Privatization of government services is a reform that has been most successful at the local level of government.

T   F   9. Today, agencies and departments of government do not play an important role in policymaking because of tight controls imposed by Congress.

T   F   10. Congress can call on the Government Accountability Office to investigate bureaucratic agencies.

Multiple Choice   Circle the correct response.

1. A basic distinction between private corporations and public bureaucracies is that private corporations
    a. have managers and public bureaucracies do not.
    b. are organized to make a profit and public bureaucracies are not.
    c. are inefficient and public bureaucracies are not.
    d. are generally large, complex enterprises, and Congress keeps public bureaucracies small.
    e. are more tightly regulated than public bureaucracies.

2. The view that top-level bureaucrats will always try to expand the size of budgets is the theory of the
    a. Weberian model.
    b. acquisitive model.
    c. monopolistic model.
    d. bureaucratic model.
    e. budget model.

3. The image of the bureaucracy as a noncompetitive organization is offered by the
    a. bureaucratic model.
    b. acquisitive model.
    c. monopolistic model.
    d. Weberian model.
    e. noncompetitive model.

4. Since 1970, most of the growth in government employment has occurred at the
    a. municipal level.
    b. state and local levels.
    c. national level.
    d. county level.
    e. sub-municipal level.

5. The two groups of people in government who may call themselves bureaucrats are
    a. members of Congress and their appointees.
    b. the president and cabinet.
    c. political appointees and civil servants.
    d. state employees and members of Congress.
    e. lobbyists and political party executives.

6. Thomas Jefferson was the first president who brought into public service
    a. a cadre of permanent civil servants.
    b. permanent patronage appointees who became professional public servants.
    c. a small ruling clique whose membership was based on birth and wealth.
    d. amateurs who were loyal servants.
    e. a group of experienced Federalists.

7. The Civil Service Reform Act (Pendleton Act) had the effect of
    a. establishing in law the spoils system for political appointment.
    b. establishing the principle of employment on the basis of open competitive exams.
    c. preventing the best-qualified people from being employed by the government.
    d. allowing corruption and graft to enter the employment practices of government.
    e. not really changing government employment.

8. The idea of sunset legislation was first suggested by President
    a. Franklin Roosevelt.
    b. Jimmy Carter.
    c. Abraham Lincoln.
    d. Ronald Reagan.
    e. George H.W. Bush.

9. The major requirement imposed by the Government in the Sunshine Act is that
    a. federal agencies and commissions can have open meetings.
    b. information on individuals and companies can be made public.
    c. secret meetings may not take place within the government.
    d. secret meetings may take place within the government.
    e. all committee-directed federal agencies conduct their business regularly in public session.

10. Sunset legislation refers to
    a. the idea that Congress must reauthorize programs annually.
    b. legislation that protects a program so that the sun will never set on the program.
    c. the idea of automatic program termination after a prescribed period unless Congress reauthorizes it.
    d. built-in protections for program continuation.
    e. legislation for solar power.

11. Congress created agencies within the federal bureaucracy to
    a. review proposed legislation.
    b. implement legislation passed by Congress.
    c. act as a sounding board for new laws.
    d. control the actions of the president.
    e. give the public an opportunity for public hearings.

12. Negotiated rulemaking involves federal agencies in negotiations with
    a. Congress.
    b. the president.
    c. the courts.
    d. parties to be affected by a new rule.
    e. the general public.

13. The iron triangle refers to
    a. a policy of controlling information through censorship.
    b. the alliance of mutual benefit formed between an agency, its client groups, and congressional committees.
    c. the mathematical formula used by the bureaucracy to determine benefit payments.
    d. an alliance between Congress, the president, and big business to control the economy.
    e. the increase in campaign contributions to presidential candidates.

14. Issue networks are
    a. another name for "iron triangles."
    b. a more complex concept than "iron triangles" that illustrates how experts support issues on a particular policy position.
    c. an attempt by the media to manipulate public opinion on a particular issue.
    d. insider relationships within Congress to protect congressional benefits.
    e. another name for political appointees.

15. The ultimate check that Congress has over the bureaucracy is the ability to
    a. hire and fire members of boards and commissions.
    b. write legislation in specific terms so that the bureaucracy will not be able to interpret the meaning of laws.
    c. withhold the appropriation of money to the bureaucracy.
    d. influence the president to take action against a bureaucrat.
    e. impeach the particular bureaucrat.

16. A person who brings public attention to government abuses is called
    a. a special abuse auditor.
    b. a member of the Government Accountability Office.
    c. a special investigator.
    d. a member of the Bureau of the President (BOP).
    e. a whistleblower.

17. Since Congress is unable to oversee the day-to-day administration of programs, it has
    a. created whistleblower legislation.
    b. enacted enabling legislation for administrative agencies.
    c. created the *Federal Register*.
    d. created issue networks.
    e. empowered more special investigative agencies.

18. Negotiated rulemaking begins when an agency publishes the subject and scope of a new rule in the
    a. broadcast media.
    b. issue networks.
    c. *Federal Register*.
    d. appropriate committee of Congress.
    e. national media.

19. Which of the following **do not** conduct investigations for Congress?
    a. congressional committees
    b. the *Federal Register*
    c. the Government Accountability Office
    d. the Congressional Budget Office
    e. the investigative issue network

20. The Congressional Review Act of 1996 provides Congress with
    a. control over bureaucratic spending.
    b. the power to force the president to negotiate issues.
    c. the power to eliminate agencies.
    d. the power to call public hearings.
    e. the ability to express disapproval of an agency.

Short Essay   Briefly address the major concepts raised by the following questions.

1. Identify and explain several theories of bureaucracy.

2. Discuss the different types of government agencies and organizations in the federal bureaucracy.

3. Describe the recent reforms in the federal civil service.

4. Explain the iron triangle and issue network models of the bureaucracy.

ANSWERS TO THE PRACTICE EXAM

Fill-in-the-Blank
1. bureaucracy
2. Weberian
3. cabinet departments
4. Independent executive agencies
5. Interstate Commerce Commission
6. government corporation
7. Andrew Jackson
8. privatization
9. iron triangle
10. enabling legislation

True/False

1. F	3. T	5. T	7. F	9. F
2. F	4. T	6. T	8. T	10. T

Multiple Choice

1. b	5. c	9. e	13. b	17. b
2. b	6. b	10. c	14. b	18. c
3. c	7. b	11. b	15. c	19. b
4. b	8. a	12. d	16. e	20. e

Short Essay
1. Identify and explain several theories of bureaucracy.
There are three basic theories: the Weberian model, the acquisitive model, and the monopolistic model.

- The classic or Weberian model views bureaucracy as a rational, hierarchical organization in which power flows from the top downward and decisions are based on logic and data.

- The acquisitive model focuses on the concept that top level bureaucrats will want to maximize the sizes of their budgets and staffs. The bureaucrat will try to "sell" the public service to Congress and the public.

- The monopolistic model emphasizes that bureaucracies are like monopolistic business firms in that they have no competition. Monopolies tend to be less efficient and more costly to operate. This model argues for the privatizing of some bureaucratic functions.

2. Discuss the different types of government agencies and organizations in the federal bureaucracy.
(See Tables 12-1, 12-2, 12-3, 12-4, and 12-5.)
There are four major types of bureaucratic structures: cabinet departments, independent executive agencies, independent regulatory agencies, and government corporations.

- Cabinet departments are the fifteen executive departments, each headed by a secretary (except for the Justice Department, which is headed by the Attorney General). These are the major service organizations of the national government.

- Independent executive agencies are federal agencies that are not part of a cabinet department but report directly to the president. An example of this kind of agency is the Central Intelligence Agency (CIA).

- Independent regulatory agencies are agencies administered independently of all three branches of government; they often perform the functions of all three branches. An example is the Federal Communication Commission (FCC), which regulates all communication by telegraph, cable, telephone, radio, and television.

- Government corporations are government agencies that administer a quasi-business enterprise. An example is the U.S. Postal Service.

3. Describe the recent reforms in the federal civil service.

The important actual and proposed recent reforms include sunshine laws, sunset laws, privatization, efficiency incentives, and more protection for whistleblowers.

- The Government in the Sunshine Act (1976) required all federal agencies headed by committee to hold public meetings.
- Sunset laws require agencies to be terminated automatically at the end of a designated period, unless specifically reauthorized. Congress has never implemented this law, but most states have passed sunset laws.
- Contracting out government services to private sector providers has been most successful at the local level, for services like trash collection.
- The Government Performance and Results Act of 1997 was designed to get government agencies to set goals and create a measurement system to document if goals were reached.
- In spite of the Whistle-Blower Protection Act of 1989, and other measures designed to encourage employees to monitor the performance and legality of their employers, individuals who bring to public attention gross governmental inefficiency or illegal action are not protected from losing their jobs.
- In 2006, the Supreme Court reversed protections in *Garcetti v. Ceballos* by affirming the punishment of a whistleblower.
- By executive order, Regulatory Policy Offices were created at all agencies in an attempt to streamline the policy implementation process.

4. Explain the iron triangle and issue network models of the bureaucracy.

The iron triangle is one way of describing the bureaucracy's role in the policy making process. It consists of a three-way alliance among legislators in Congress, bureaucrats, and interest groups in a given policy area. Some examples are agricultural policy, weapon systems policy, and crime policy.

The concept of issue networks is a more complex way to describe the bureaucracy's role in the policy making process. An issue network comprises individuals or groups of experts that support a particular policy position on a given issue. This includes scholars, media, and others not usually considered part of the iron triangle theory.

Chapter 13
THE COURTS

CHAPTER SUMMARY

Most American law has its base in the common law tradition of England, in which the decisions of judges are a vital part of lawmaking. This has influenced the U.S. courts system and is the source of much of the judiciary's policymaking power explored in this chapter.

The Common Law Tradition

The concept of common law originated in England as judge-made law that grew out of judicial decisions shaped by prevailing custom. This concept has influenced the American judicial system. The two main components of common law are precedent, which is a court decision that will bear on subsequent cases, and *stare decisis*, which means to stand on decided cases. Judges, then, are obliged to look to previous decisions of courts and also to follow the decisions of higher courts.

Sources of American Law

The major sources of American law are federal and state constitutions, statutes passed by legislative bodies, administrative law, and case law. Constitutions set forth the general organization, powers, and limits of government. The U.S. Constitution is the supreme law of the land. Statutes or ordinances (and administrative law) passed by national, state, and local governments have increasingly become important as courts apply these concepts to the general framework of common law. Case law involves the judicial interpretations of rules and principles announced in court decisions pertaining to constitutional law, statutory law, and administrative law; through interpretations, then, courts effectively establish law.

The Federal Court System

The United States has a dual court system made up of the federal court structure and the courts of the fifty states and the District of Columbia (a total of 52 court systems). In any court system, requirements of jurisdiction and standing to sue must be met. Jurisdiction is important because not all courts have the authority to decide all cases. The federal system has limited jurisdiction under Article III, Section 1, of the Constitution; it can try cases of federal questions or when there is a diversity of citizenship in the suit. A party bringing suit must also stand to sue and demonstrate both that they have sufficient stake in the matter and that the issue presents a justiciable controversy. The federal court system is a three-tiered pyramid. (See Figure 13-1.) Cases start in U.S. district courts or courts of limited jurisdiction (like bankruptcy court), which are the trial courts. Parties who lose at this level can appeal to the circuit court of appeals (or appellate court), at which "trial" involves court review and attorney argument rather than the previous procedure of witnesses and juries. Appellate courts look at questions of law rather than questions of fact. (See Figure 13-2 for the geographic boundaries of federal district courts and circuit courts of appeals.) Parties who lose at the circuit court level can appeal their case to the United States Supreme Court, but only some cases are determined by the Supreme Court to be worthy of review. The Supreme Court can try original cases, but it serves mostly as the highest appellate court for both federal court cases as well as state supreme court rulings on federal matters. Finally, there are some specialized, secret federal courts that have taken on great significance in the war against terrorism. The Foreign Intelligence Surveillance Act (FISA) was enacted in 1978 to authorize surveillance on spies in situations that needed to involve a greater level of secrecy than normal criminal cases. After 9/11 these FISA courts were given even greater latitude to authorize surveillance on terrorist suspects. An alien "removal court" was created by Congress after the 1995 Oklahoma City bombing and has also become another tool in the fight against terrorism. The creation of the Guantanamo Bay prison camp for enemy combatants has lead to heated political debates. The Supreme Court twice determined that their treatment violated the U.S. Constitution and specifically the right of *habeas corpus*. Congress then removed the Court's ability to regulate their treatment with the Military Commissions Act of 2006. In 2008, the Court ruled that denial of detainee's *habeas corpus* rights was illegal. When any case comes before a court, the two parties in a lawsuit are the plaintiff, who initiates the suit, and the defendant, the party against whom the suit is brought. Note that interest groups can litigate, or bring the case to trial, and influence the judicial process by filing *amicus curiae* briefs expressing a group's viewpoint on the case. Class-action suits are also brought by groups to benefit all citizens who are similarly situated in the harm they have suffered. Federal and state courts alike have procedural rules that shape the process of litigation and ensure a smoothly functioning, nonpartisan trial. Parties who fail to follow rules face charges of civil or criminal contempt.

The Supreme Court at Work

The Supreme Court term begins on the first Monday in October and lasts until late June or early July. The Court sets its own agenda, thereby exercising a great deal of influence over the nation's policies through its decisions about which cases to hear and which to let stand. Several factors affect the Court's decision to hear a case. The Supreme Court only considers cases involving significant issues affecting public policy. If lower federal courts have ruled in a contradictory manner on constitutional questions, there will be pressure for the Supreme Court to resolve the conflict. Frequently, the Court is responsive to the case recommendations of the solicitor general of the United States, who represents the government in cases before the Supreme Court. When the Court does grant a petition to review, it issues a *writ of certiorari* to have the case record sent up. A writ is issued only if at least four justices approve, in what is called the rule of four and only a very small percentage of cases are finally accepted. If the Court takes the case on, the first step is extensive judicial research on the case. The Court does not hear evidence, but attorneys do present oral arguments. Then the justices meet in conference to discuss the arguments and decide the case. The Court can affirm or reverse the lower court's ruling or remand the case back to the lower court. The Supreme Court does not simply decide a case; it explains its opinion, and the explanation presented frequently has a greater impact than the decision itself. When all the justices agree, they issue a unanimous opinion. In absence of agreement, the majority opinion is issued by the justices in the majority on the case. If a member of the Court agrees with the result reached by the majority opinion but disagrees with the reasoning employed, that member can write a concurring opinion. Finally, those members of the Court who disagree with the majority completely can write a dissenting opinion, in which they signal to the legal community and to the nation their belief that the Court made a mistake in this case and their hope that parties will challenge this precedent. Ultimately, the opinion is published in the official printed record of Supreme Court decisions, the *United States Reports*. Many have criticized the Court for its dwindling caseload. For example, in the 1982-83 term, the Court issued 151 decisions. This number has dropped by more than half to 69 in the 2006 term.

The Selection of Federal Judges

All federal judges are appointed by the president with the advice and consent of the Senate. The concept of senatorial courtesy allows a senator from the president's political party to exercise influence over the nomination of federal district court judges in his or her state. Making appointments to the Supreme Court ranks among the most important actions taken by a president. (See Table 13-1 for the background of Supreme Court justices.) Ideology plays a major role in the selection process for federal judges. Most presidents select judges from their own political party who share their own ideology. Bill Clinton selected more women and members of minority groups to federal judgeships than any president before him. Clinton also appointed two of the Supreme Court's more left-leaning justices, Ruth Bader Ginsburg and Stephen Breyer. George W. Bush had the opportunity to appoint the Chief Justice of the Supreme Court, John Roberts. After his initial nomination for a second seat, Harriet Miers, was the target of criticism from Republicans in the Senate, Bush appointed Samuel Alito to become the Court's newest member. The Senate's role in judicial appointments can also reflect ideology, and the Senate has a long history of refusing to confirm the president's nominations. The 1990s and 2000s have proven to be very partisan in terms of Senate battles over nominees.

Policymaking and the Courts

With its power of judicial review—the authority to consider the constitutionality of the actions of Congress, the president, the bureaucracy and state and local governments—the Supreme Court is a major player in determining the direction of the nation. Article III of the Constitution states that the judicial power will be placed in a Supreme Court, and many argue that the Framers thus intended the concept of judicial power to include judicial review. The practice was formally established in the Supreme Court's decision in *Marbury v. Madison* (1803). There are dramatically different views of the Court's role in policymaking. Some hold that the Supreme Court should take an active role in using its powers to check the other institutions of government when they exceed their authority, in judicial activism. Judicial restraint, however, rests on the principle that the Court should defer to the decisions made by the institutions elected by the people. Also, a justice's decisions can be viewed as either following a strict construction or a broad construction of the Constitution. Often, both judicial activism and broad constructionism are associated with "liberal" judges, but this is not universally the case. The Court under Supreme Justice William H. Rehnquist is a good example of the ideologies of the justices leading the Court, and thus the nation. Beginning with the 1986 confirmation of Rehnquist as Chief Justice, the Supreme Court began an ideological shift in one direction (right, or conservative, in this case). As the Court began to take increasingly conservative stances, an ideological counter-response occurred that made many of the rulings from the Rehnquist period seemingly contradictory. In one ruling, the rights of the federal government were expanded, in another ruling, the Court contradicted itself by eliminating federal powers. It is suggested that during this period some previously conservative justices showed a tendency to mitigate to a more liberal view of the law in response to the conservative shift, thus leading to mixed rulings. These justices are called the "swing votes." This transition period came to an end with the 2005 confirmation of John Roberts as the new Chief Justice. Although the current Supreme Court (see Figure 13-3) is sharply divided in its philosophical composition, it is strongly conservative. Under Robert's leadership the Court has taken very conservative stances on issues such as abortion, environmentalism, executive power, gun ownership, the death penalty and criminal rights. Among other conservative rulings, the Court has upheld a ban on partial birth abortions, has limited the freedom of speech for high school students and has placed inflexible deadlines on the time limitations for an employee's ability to sue for pay discrimination. Justice Kennedy remains the last "swing" vote that is currently mitigating the continued conservative shift.

What Checks Our Courts?

Though the American judicial system is one of the world's most independent, the executive branch, the legislature, the public, and the judiciary itself all can check the power of the courts. The president's most direct control is through the appointment of new judges. Also, since the executive branch carries out judicial rulings, the courts' lack of judicial implementation can also serve as an check on the judiciary. A key congressional check on the courts lies in the fact that the legislature is in charge of the funding required to carry out rulings. Congress can also amend the Constitution or, more simply, pass new laws to overturn a court's ruling (the Civil Rights Act of 1991 is an example of a law passed to check the courts). States can also pass laws that negate Supreme Court rulings. Public opinion can limit the power of courts since they have no enforcement powers; its authority is linked to its stature in the eyes of the public and those who disagree with a ruling can ignore it (as in the unconstitutional but still performed school prayer). The Supreme Court, too, is influenced by the *zeitgeist* in which it operates. Finally, the Supreme Court (as well as other courts) also tends to control itself through precedent and tradition. The Court exercises discretion in the cases it chooses to hear and can send a case to an elected branch of government if it finds the question to be political rather than justiciable. Lower courts, subject to reversals from higher courts, can check those higher courts as well by indirect means such as broad interpretations of Supreme Court rulings in specific lower court cases.

KEY TERMS

affirm	judicial activism
amicus curiae brief	judicial implementation
appellate court	judicial restraint
broad construction	jurisdiction
case law	limited jurisdiction
class-action suit	litigate
common law	majority opinion
concurring opinion	opinion
dissenting opinion	oral arguments
diversity of citizenship	political question
federal question	precedent
general jurisdiction	remand

reverse
rule of four
senatorial courtesy
stare decisis

strict construction
trial court
unanimous opinion
writ of certiorari

OTHER RESOURCES

A number of valuable supplements are available to students using the Schmidt, Shelley, and Bardes text. A list of suggested supplements is at the end of the chapter. Ask your instructor how to obtain these resources. One supplement is highlighted here, the Web site of the U.S. Supreme Court.

E-MOCRACY EXERCISES

Direct URL: http://www.supremecourtus.gov/opinions/08slipopinion.html

Surfing Instructions:
Log on to www.supremecourtus.gov
Click on "Recent Decisions."
Select any case from the list.

Study Questions
1. In this case who was the plaintiff and defendant?
2. What is the Constitutional controversy they are debating?
3. How many justices were in the majority opinion versus the dissenting opinion?
4. What was the majority's ruling?

PRACTICE EXAM
(Answers appear at the end of this chapter.)

Fill-in-the-Blank   Supply the missing word(s) or term(s) to complete the sentence.

1. The body of judge-made law that developed in England and is still used today in the United States is called
    _____ _____.

2. The practice of deciding new cases with reference to former decisions is based upon the doctrine of
    _____ _____.

3. The United States' dual court system consists of both _____ courts and _____ courts.

4. The Supreme Court's decision to hear a case is determined by the _____ ____ _____.

5. A _____ suit, filed by an individual, seeks damages for "all persons similarly situated."

6. By _____ _____ _____ the Supreme Court orders a lower court to send it the record of a case for review.

7. A _____ opinion is an opinion written by a Supreme Court justice who agrees with the majority opinion but for different reasons.

8. About 20% of Supreme Court appointments are _____ by the Senate.

9. Court decisions are translated into action by _____ _____.

10. Justices following the doctrine of _____ _____ believe the Supreme Court should defer to decisions made by elected representatives.

True/False   Circle the appropriate letter to indicate if the statement is true or false.

T   F   1.   Most of American law is based on the English legal system.

T   F   2.   Case law includes judicial interpretations of common law.

T   F   3.   Federal court jurisdiction is less limited than state court jurisdiction because the federal government has jurisdiction over all the country.

T   F   4.   Federal courts have authority to rule on all issues relating to state laws and federal matters.

T   F   5.   Interest groups no longer use *amicus curiae* briefs to influence Supreme Court decisions.

T   F   6.   Federal judges are either appointed or elected depending upon the type of court.

T   F   7.   The nomination of Supreme Court justices belongs solely to the president.

T   F   8.   Ideology no longer plays a very important role in a president's choice for the Supreme Court.

T   F   9.   The makeup of the federal judiciary is typical of the American public.

T   F   10. John Roberts is the current Chief Justice.

Multiple Choice   Circle the correct response.

1.   *Stare decisis* is a doctrine that
     a.   enables court decisions to vary from case to case.
     b.   provides guidance to judges when common law does not apply.
     c.   encourages the following of precedent, or previous court decisions.
     d.   requires hearings about complaints arising from regulations.
     e.   applies only to the U.S. Supreme Court.

2.   The level of trial courts in the federal judicial hierarchy is the
     a.   district court.
     b.   court of appeals.
     c.   Supreme Court.
     d.   state court.
     e.   trial court.

3.   Appellate jurisdiction refers to the authority of a court to
     a.   serve as a trial court.
     b.   hear cases for the first time.
     c.   review decisions from a lower court.
     d.   establish grand juries.
     e.   serve as an administrative court.

4.   A *writ of certiorari* is an order
     a.   compelling an official to carry out his responsibilities.
     b.   guaranteeing the right to a fair and impartial trial by jury.
     c.   preventing some action from being carried out.
     d.   to a lower court to send a case to the higher court for review.
     e.   to require bail for an individual accused of a crime.

5. A *writ of certiorari* is issued by the Supreme Court only when
    a. a majority of justices vote for such a request.
    b. four justices vote for such a request.
    c. a unanimous Court supports such a request.
    d. the solicitor general approves such a request.
    e. the death penalty is involved.

6. The official who represents the national government in the Supreme Court is the
    a. attorney general.
    b. solicitor general.
    c. vice president.
    d. chief justice.
    e. secretary of state.

7. A justice who accepts the majority decision, but not the reasons for it, may write a(n)
    a. minority opinion.
    b. majority opinion.
    c. *amicus curiae* opinion.
    d. concurring opinion.
    e. individual opinion.

8. In terms of enforcement powers, the Supreme Court
    a. has now acquired a police force.
    b. relies upon the goodwill of the public to see that its decisions are enforced.
    c. must rely on other units of government to carry out its decisions.
    d. does not make decisions that have to be enforced.
    e. can go public, and use public opinion to enforce the opinion.

9. Dissenting opinions in a Supreme Court decision are important because
    a. they allow justices to make symbolic statements.
    b. they agree with the majority opinion, but for different reasons.
    c. they often form the basis for arguments that reverse decisions and establish new precedents.
    d. they allow opposition groups to express their opinions before the Court.
    e. they may cause a rehearing of the case.

10. Senatorial courtesy
    a. allows the president to pick his choice for judge.
    b. allows a senator to veto a president's choice for judge.
    c. applies only to Supreme Court nominations.
    d. applies only to state court nominations.
    e. is never used in the Senate.

11. The courts that have become "stepping stones" to appointment to the Supreme Court are the
    a. district courts.
    b. state supreme courts.
    c. federal courts of appeals.
    d. tax courts.
    e. federal security courts.

12. Anthony Kennedy often functions in the Supreme Court as a
    a. liberal justice.
    b. swing vote.
    c. conservative justice.
    d. libertarian justice.
    e. radical individual rights justice.

13. The justices who believe that the Court should use its power to alter or challenge the policy direction of Congress, state legislatures, or administrative agencies are advocating
    a. judicial restraint.
    b. judicial activism.
    c. strict constructionism.
    d. moderate pragmatism.
    e. judicial awareness.

14. The tradition of the Court has led justices to refuse to hear cases which are
    a. justiciable disputes.
    b. political questions.
    c. between citizens of different states.
    d. real controversies.
    e. interpreting the Constitution.

15. The appointments of President Clinton to the Supreme Court have elevated the number of
    a. women to record numbers.
    b. Democrats to record numbers.
    c. libertarian members to record numbers.
    d. liberal members to record numbers.
    e. conservative members to record numbers.

16. Case law refers to
    a. a case involving federal law.
    b. a case heard by the Supreme Court.
    c. rules and principles announced in court decisions.
    d. a justiciable dispute.
    e. a case involving state law.

17. The concept of judicial review was established in
    a. *Marbury v. Madison*.
    b. *McCulloch v. Maryland*.
    c. common law.
    d. *Brown v. Board of Education of Topeka*.
    e. the Judicial Review Act of 2000.

18. With the confirmation of Roberts, the Court has continued its _____ approach to issues such as abortion, environmentalism, executive power and criminal rights.
    a. liberal
    b. conservative
    c. state's rights
    d. anti-federalist
    e. progressive

19. Judicial implementation is
    a. the Court enforcing its decision.
    b. the way in which court decisions are translated into action.
    c. a dispute that arises out of actual cases.
    d. a case decided by the Supreme Court.
    e. a ruling by Congress.

20. The rulings of the U.S. Supreme Court during the Rehnquist period surprised many observers because
    a. some previously liberal justices acted as conservative swing votes.
    b. the Court maintained an ideologically consistent voting record.
    c. the Court shifted its ideology to a liberal stance.
    d. some previously conservative justices acted as liberal swing votes.
    e. the Court shifted its ideology to a progressive stance.

Short Essay   Briefly address the major concepts raised by the following questions.

1. Identify and explain the common law tradition and other major sources of American law.

2. Discuss the process the Supreme Court uses to select and decide cases.

3. Describe the presidential appointment process for federal judges.

4. Explain the checks or limitations on the power of the federal courts.

ANSWERS TO THE PRACTICE EXAM

Fill-in-the-Blank
1. common law
2. *stare decisis*
3. state, federal
4. rule of four
5. class-action
6. *writ of certiorari*
7. concurring
8. rejected
9. judicial implementation
10. judicial restraint

True/False

1. T	3. T	5. F	7. T	9. F
2. T	4. F	6. F	8. F	10. T

Multiple Choice

1. c	5. b	9. c	13. b	17. a
2. a	6. b	10. b	14. b	18. b
3. c	7. d	11. c	15. a	19. b
4. d	8. c	12. b	16. c	20. d

Short Essay

1.   Identify and explain the common law tradition and other major sources of American law.
Common law is a body of judge-made law that originated in England from decisions shaped according to prevailing custom.
The other major sources of American law are federal and state constitutions, statutes, administrative law, and case law.
Constitutions set forth the general organization, powers, and limits of government.
Statutes are laws enacted by any legislative body at federal, state, or local levels.
Rules and regulations issued by administrative agencies are a source of law.
Case law includes judicial interpretations of all of the above sources of law.

2.   Discuss the process the Supreme Court uses to select and decide cases.

The Supreme Court term begins in October and usually adjourns in June or July.

The first important decision for the Court is to decide which cases to hear. Important factors to consider are whether a legal issue has been decided differently by two separate courts and if the Solicitor General is pushing the case.

If the Court decides to hear a case, four justices (the rule of four) must agree to issue a *writ of certiorari*.

Oral arguments, in which attorneys representing each side will present their cases, will be scheduled before the Court.

A private conference will be held in which the justices discuss and decide a case.

Opinions can be unanimous, majority, concurring, and dissenting.

3.   Describe the presidential appointment process for federal judges.

All federal judges are appointed for life terms by the president, with Senate advice and consent.

The first step in the process is nomination by the president.

Senatorial courtesy can be a big factor in the nomination of federal district judges. A senator of the president's party has a great deal of influence over federal district judge appointments from the senator's state.

Ideology and political party background are two of the most important factors determining who is nominated for federal judgeships.

4.   Explain the checks or limitations on the power of the federal courts.

Our judicial system is probably the most independent in the world, but there are important checks on the power of the courts. These checks fall under the categories of executive, legislative, public, and of the judiciary itself.

The executive branch has the power of judicial implementation. The way in which court decisions are translated into action is solely the responsibility of the executive branch.

Congress can modify or overturn court rulings through lack of appropriations to carry out their rulings, or by constitutional amendments that nullify a ruling.

Public opinion is an important factor. Since the Court has no enforcement powers, its authority is linked to its stature in the eyes of the public.

Federal judges typically exercise self-restraint in making their decisions. Political questions are issues that a court defers to the decision-making of the executive or legislative branches.

Chapter 14
DOMESTIC AND ECONOMIC POLICY

CHAPTER SUMMARY

All policymaking involves the central dilemma that some groups will be left better off and some groups will be hurt. In this chapter we explore the domestic and economic policy of the U.S. and the many tradeoffs involved in setting out the path of daily life in America.

The Policymaking Process

The beginning of the policymaking process is the recognition that a problem exists and needs a solution. There are five basic steps in policymaking: 1) agenda building, 2) policy formation, 3) policy adoption, 4) policy implementation, and 5) policy evaluation. First, an agenda is built when Congress becomes aware that an issue requires action, whether by media or lobbyist attention or through a crisis or technological change. Next, policy is formulated through discussions among bureaucrats and the public. A policy will then be adopted from the many proposed options. Congress implements the new policy and the bureaucrats, courts, police, and citizens all implement the government action. Lastly, after a policy has been in effect for some time, it faces evaluation from groups inside and outside the government to determine the success or failure of the policy and to see what policy changes might be necessary. In the case of evaluating the U.S. Farm Bill, Congress is currently debating if the government should expand or limit federal subsidies to U.S. farmers. Since 1970, these subsidies have exceeded $650 billion.

Health Care

Spending for health care is estimated at almost 16% of the total U.S. economy and represents a hefty percentage of the gross domestic product (GDP) of the country. (See Figures 14-1 and 14-2.) The rising cost of health care can be attributed to a number of factors including: increasing life expectancies which naturally lead to an aging population (see Figure 14-3), advanced and expensive technology, and soaring costs associated with government involvement in health care through the Medicare and Medicaid programs. The Medicare program, created in 1965 under President Lyndon Johnson, pays hospital and doctor bills for U.S. residents over the age of 65. Medicare is second only to Social Security in domestic spending. Some government responses to such high costs have been reimbursement caps and a reduction in payment to hospitals and doctors. As a result, more doctors are refusing to accept Medicare patients. The Medicaid program is designed to provide health care for the "working poor" and has generated one of the biggest expansions of government entitlements in the last fifty years. One reason behind this expansion is that the ceiling for eligibility has been raised, so more people are eligible for and are choosing the often better care that Medicaid can provide. Over 47 million Americans—sixteen percent of the population—do not have health insurance. This number varies greatly from state to state and includes many individuals who are employed but cannot afford insurance. The uninsured often pay the highest prices for hospitals and doctors. Indeed, the United States remains the only western, industrialized nation that does not provide National Health Insurance. In such a program, private insurers are excluded from providing basic health coverage and all citizens are covered under one plan. In 2003, Republicans introduced Health Care Savings Accounts (HSAs) which permitted individuals to save a portion of their paychecks aside tax-free. This money could then be used to pay for their health care costs. Some of the challenges to this system are that it does not provide universal coverage and assumes that individuals have extra money to set aside. Recent calls have been for the creation of a universal heath care system similar to systems used in every other country.

Poverty and Welfare

The U.S. has a very high standard of living globally speaking, so the poverty that persists here can seem incongruous. Industrialized, wealthy nations like the United States have been able to mitigate mass poverty through income transfers. (See Figure 14-4 for the official number of poor in the United States; note that the ways the "poor" are determined have changed over time.) The official definition of poverty in the United States in 2008 for a family of four is an income of around $21,000 a year. In-kind subsidies such as food stamps, low-income housing, and medical care are not usually counted as income. An array of government programs attempt to transfer income from wealthy to poor individuals, but it is difficult to determine just which programs constitute antipoverty measures. In the wake of the Welfare Reform Act of 1996, Temporary Assistance to Needy Families (TANF) is the central basic welfare measure. The TANF program gives block grants to states to administer welfare assistance and replaced the Aid to Families with Dependent Children (AFDC) program. Both programs have been controversial, with conservatives and libertarians raising the strongest objections. The government also assists the working poor through Supplemental Security Income (SSI), food stamps, and the earned-income tax credit (EITC) program. Homelessness, which is intertwined with and related to poverty, is still a problem in the U.S. It is difficult to estimate the number of homeless people because some are street people, who tend to be single and sleep outside, while others are sheltered homeless, a group which includes families who sleep in overnight facilities. There is much disagreement over the reasons for and solutions to homelessness, with conflict again between conservatives and liberals.

Immigration

Immigration is a constant force in American society and politics; Americans and their leaders face questions about the effect of immigration and about the negative or positive influence of immigrants. Today, immigration rates are among the highest they have been since their peak in the early twentieth century. Immigrants are becoming an increasingly important group and if trends continue, the many minorities will collectively make up the majority of Americans by 2060, wielding considerable power. One advantage of a high rate of immigration is that it offsets a low birth rate and aging population, two characteristics of today's U.S. There are many groups with the opinion that legal and—even more so—illegal immigration both have a negative impact, depressing wages and overloading schools and hospitals. In 2006 and 2007, the president called for a massive overhaul of the laws dealing with illegal immigrants. In 2006, reform efforts were met with mass demonstrations in support of immigrants throughout the country (especially from the Hispanic community). Congress' response was mixed and contentious. Some members put forth measures that would make all illegal immigrants felons while others proposed a path to citizenship; the latter program had President George W. Bush's support. The two houses of Congress have been unable to reach a reform agreement. They did, however, pass legislation authorizing the creation of a 700 mile fence for the U.S.-Mexico boarder.

Crime in the Twenty-First Century

Though crime rates may rise and fall, polls show that crime has been a major and constant concern of Americans in every period of our history. Mob violence abounded before the Civil War; in the decades from 1860 to 1890, the crime rate rose twice as fast as the population. The 1900s to 1930s saw a dramatic crime increase; only from the mid-1930s to the 1960s did crime begin to go down for the first time in history. Violent crime is of special concern to Americans, and though the U.S. does not have the highest overall crime rate of developed countries, the murder rate is unusually high. (See Figures 14-5, 14-6, and 14-7 for profiles of violent crime over time.) Crimes committed by juveniles are particularly troubling, and though the rates are dropping (see Figure 14-8), some fear that the decrease is temporary. One of the most difficult crimes to understand are school shootings. Occurring in virtually every school setting, their frequency is alarming. The number of people in correctional facilities has grown rapidly since the 1990s and by 2007, 2.2 million people were being held in jails and prisons. Certain groups have higher incarceration rates than others: men more than women, African Americans more than everyone else (see Figure 14-9). These incarceration rates are very hard on the families left behind and, in particular, their children. For black children, ten percent have a father in prison. The U.S. has the highest overall incarceration rate in the world (see Figure 14-10 for comparisons) and most facilities operate over capacity. This overcrowding is combined with other chronic prison problems such as prison violence, disease and untreated mental illness. The federal war on drugs (and its attendant spending) has had almost no effect on drug consumption in the U.S.; rather, its greatest effect has been to pack the prison system. Some states are changing tactics to favor "drug courts" with rehabilitation sentencing. Finally, terrorism is now a major crime concern for the first time in America. Combating terrorism has far-reaching implications with issues such as the continuing war in Iraq and the use of warrantless wiretaps.

Environmental Policy

The last three decades have seen increased attention drawn to environmental issues, especially pollution. The first major environmental legislation, prompted by the Santa Barbara oil spill in 1969, was the National

Environmental Policy Act. This act established the Council on Environmental Quality and required the preparation of environmental impact statements (EIS) for major federal actions that might affect the quality of the environment. The Clean Air Act of 1990 addressed motor vehicle emissions (a major concern for cities), set greater regulations on coal power plants and factories, and ended the production of chlorofluorocarbons. The Clean Water Act of 1972 amended a prior act from 1948 and had the stated goals of making water safe for swimming, protecting fish and wildlife, and eliminating pollution discharge into the water. It also extends certain protections to wetlands; these protections have been debated and altered over time. In the 1990s one of the most controversial environmental issues was global warming. The 1997 Kyoto Protocol was a worldwide effort to reduce emissions of greenhouse gases; the U.S. Senate unanimously voted to reject the treaty. By 2007, 124 nations had ratified the protocol but even some supporters are falling short of their pledged goals. Additionally, global warming is still a matter of debate among some who are not sure how large the warming effects will be, with lower estimates of 0.75 degrees Celsius and high figures of 4.5 degrees Celsius. The matter is also a great political football. As discussed previously, the Supreme Court recently forced the EPA to regulate greenhouse gasses and, in particular, carbon dioxide emissions.

The Politics of Economic Decision Making

The government faces important questions of economic policy, particularly over fiscal and monetary policy. Fiscal policy is associated with Congress and is often influenced by the work of John Maynard Keynes, whose work supports the idea that government taxing and spending should be used to help stabilize the economy, especially in the case of an economic recession. His ideas developed during the Great Depression and required that the government spend borrowed money rather than revenue generated by taxes, thus creating a budget deficit. The government borrows by selling U.S. Treasury bonds to corporations, individuals, pension plans, and even foreign governments and individuals (who now own 50 percent of U.S. public debt). The two types of public debt are the gross public debt and the net public debt. (See Figure 14-11 and Figure 14-12, the latter of which compares net debt to GDP.) The federal government has operated at a deficit from 1960 to the present with the only exception being the period of federal surplus from 1998 to 2002. For example, the fiscal year of 2007 operated with an estimated $162 billion dollar deficit. 2008 is estimated to have a deficit of $410 billion. The Federal Reserve System (or Fed) is in charge of the monetary policy of the U.S.; it manages the rate of growth in the money supply by regulating the amount of money in circulation, transferring checks among banks, and holding the reserves deposited by most of the nation's financial institutions. The most important part of the Fed is the Federal Open Market Committee, which determines the future growth of the money supply. The Fed can implement a loose monetary policy, in which the supply of credit will increase and its cost fall, or a tight monetary policy, in which the opposite happens. Results of changes in fiscal and monetary policies are often not immediate and this time lag makes predictions and analysis difficult.

The Politics of Taxes

Americans pay a variety of different taxes. (See Figure 14-13 for how the U.S. ranks with other countries in the percent of taxes. See Table 14-1 for 2007 marginal tax rates.) Individuals and corporations facing high taxes will have a big incentive to find or add loopholes to the tax laws. Tax cuts have been a major part of President George W. Bush's plan to stimulate the economy. Some taxes are progressive, with higher percentage rates for higher incomes, while others are regressive and fall in percentage as income rises (See Table 14-2 for the nature of different taxes). Taxes are a political question because policymakers have control over the tax code and can alter the progressiveness or regressiveness of taxes, therefore changing the relative impact of taxes for the rich and poor.

The Social Security Problem

The question of Social Security comes on the heels of discussions of taxation. The tax that funds Social Security is regressive at 6.2 percent on each employee's wages, up to $94,200. Rather than being a pension fund, Social Security is a system in which those who are working pay benefits to those who are retired, but the number of people working relative to the number who are retired is shrinking (see Figure 14-15). The glut of retiring baby boomers exacerbates this problem, as does the increasing cost of medical care. Proposals to salvage Social Security have included generating more taxes, both by raising the tax rate and by eliminating the $94,200 cap; increasing the age of full eligibility; permitting into the country more working immigrants who would then pay into the system; and partially privatizing the system with the goal of increasing the rate of return on retirement contributions. In 2004, President Bush proposed privatizing social security but was met with heavy resistance and ultimately his reforms were not implemented.

World Trade

World trade is a controversial topic; while it enjoys the support of economists from all points on the political spectrum, the general public feels that increased international trade hurts U.S. workers and companies. Results from Gallup polls argue that nearly two-thirds of respondents believe that international trade hurts U.S. workers. About half believe that it hurts U.S. companies. Today, about 17 percent of the goods and services purchased by Americans are imports. America sends over $1 trillion in exports, constituting about 11 percent of the GDP. In addition, the U.S. exports about $490 billion of services. World trade has become more important for the U.S and the world. (See Figure 14-16.) Some groups of nations have formed free trade areas, like that created by NAFTA, or common markets, like the European Union, to eliminate trade restrictions among member nations. The World Trade Organization was created in 1997 as the chief body that oversees tariffs worldwide; it administers trade agreements, provides a forum for negotiation, settles trade disputes, and reviews trade policy. It also draws the negative attention of opponents of globalization, who fear that the WTO could weaken environmental, health, and consumer safety laws if those laws stood in the way of trade.

KEY TERMS

budget deficit
domestic policy
earned-income tax credit (EITC) program
environmental impact statement (EIS)
exports
Federal Open Market Committee
Federal Reserve System (the Fed)
fiscal policy
food stamps
gross domestic product (GDP)
gross public debt
imports
incarceration rate
income transfer
in-kind subsidy
Keynesian economics

loophole
loose monetary policy
Medicaid
Medicare
monetary policy
National Health Insurance
net public debt
progressive tax
recession
regressive tax
Supplemental Security Income (SSI)
tariff
Temporary Assistance to Needy Families (TANF)
tight monetary policy
Universal Health Insurance
U.S. Treasury bond

OTHER RESOURCES

A number of valuable supplements are available to students using the Schmidt, Shelley, and Bardes text. A list of suggested supplements is at the end of the chapter. Ask your instructor how to obtain these resources. One supplement is highlighted here, U.S. Census poverty rates.

E-MOCRACY EXERCISES

Direct URL: http://www.census.gov/hhes/www/poverty/histpov/famindex.html

Surfing Instructions:
Log on to www.census.gov/hhes/www/poverty.html
Under "Current Poverty Data" select "Historical Tables"
Select "Families"
Click on "Table 4."

Study Questions
1.   Since 1959 has the percentage of "all families" living in poverty remained stable, decreased or increased?
2.   Since 1959 has the percentage of "married families" living in poverty remained stable, decreased or increased?
3.   Now go back and click on "Table 13." Why do you think the poverty rate for "families with a female householder" is three time higher than the poverty rate for "all families"?

PRACTICE EXAM
(Answers appear at the end of this chapter.)

Fill-in-the-Blank   Supply the missing word(s) or term(s) to complete the sentence.

1.   Courses of action on issues of national importance are called _____ _____.

2.   Selecting a specific strategy in the policymaking process is referred to as _____ _____.

3.   A traditional solution to poverty has been _____ _____.

4.   A disturbing element of crime in the U.S. is the number of serious crimes committed by _____.

5.   The majority of arrests today in the U.S. are for crimes related to _____ _____.

6.   The major environmental law prompted by the Santa Barbara oil spill was the _____
_____ _____ _____.

7.   One of the most significant environmental issues to develop in the last few years is _____
_____.

8.   The economic theory associated with using fiscal policy to alter national economic variables is
called _____ _____.

9.   The Social Security system is a pay-as-you-go transfer system in which those who are _____
pay benefits to those who are _____.

10.   The organization created to lessen trade barriers throughout the world is the _____ _____
_____.

True/False   Circle the appropriate letter to indicate if the statement is true or false.

T   F   1.   The first step in the policymaking process is getting the issue on the agenda.

T   F   2.   The poverty rate for a family of four is approximately $21,000.

T   F   3.   Food stamps are given only to the elderly and disabled.

T   F   4.   The problem of homelessness has almost disappeared in the 21st century.

T   F   5.   Polls indicate that most Americans are worried about violent crime.

T   F   6.   Only recently has the U.S. government begun to respond to the problems of pollution.

T   F   7.   The United States is making fairly substantial strides in the war on toxic emissions.

T   F   8.   The Kyoto Protocol signed by the United States is helping to solve the problem of global warming.

T   F   9.   When the economy is in a recession, the Federal Reserve Board will usually increase the amount of money in circulation.

T   F   10.   Recent talks involving the World Trade Organization have ended with controversy between developed and developing nations.

Multiple Choice   Circle the correct response.

1. The first step in solving a public problem is
    a.   to determine the cost involved.
    b.   to determine who will be helped and who will be harmed.
    c.   for people to become aware of the problem.
    d.   for the president to declare a state of emergency.
    e.   to finance the project.

2. After public policy implementation, the last step is
    a.   the variables associated with cost analysis.
    b.   policy evaluation.
    c.   policy accomplishment.
    d.   policy formulation.
    e.   policy adoption.

3. The United States has been able to eliminate mass poverty because of
    a.   foreign aid from other countries.
    b.   sustained economic growth.
    c.   an increased work ethic.
    d.   mass infusions of tax dollars.
    e.   low-income tax cuts.

4. The threshold income level for defining poverty was originally based on
    a.   the Gross Domestic Product (GDP).
    b.   the annual price changes in food.
    c.   guidelines established by the Consumer Protection Agency.
    d.   guidelines from the Farmers Union.
    e.   guidelines from the Office of Management and Budget.

5. If the official poverty level were adjusted to include food stamps and housing vouchers, it would
    a.   significantly increase the number of people classified as living below the poverty line.
    b.   dramatically lower the percentage of the population below the poverty line.
    c.   only marginally lower the percentage of the population above the poverty line.
    d.   effectively reduce the level of benefits.
    e.   have no impact on the poverty level.

6. The Welfare Reform Act of 1996 (Personal Responsibility and Work Opportunity Reconciliation Act) gave more control over welfare to
    a.   the national bureaucracy.
    b.   state governments.
    c.   local government.
    d.   the private sector.
    e.   faith-based groups.

7. During the first five years of welfare reform, families receiving benefits declined by
    a.   20 percent.
    b.   30 percent.
    c.   40 percent.
    d.   45 percent.
    e.   50 percent.

8. The National Environmental Policy Act created the
    a. requirement of environmental impact statements.
    b. Clean Air Act.
    c. ozone limits.
    d. Clean Water Act.
    e. ban on global warming.

9. What part of the Clean Water Act of 1972 did the Supreme Court rule unconstitutional in 2001?
    a. The goal to make waters safe for swimming
    b. The protection of fish and wildlife
    c. The elimination of the discharge of pollutants into the water
    d. The filling or dredging of wetlands without a permit
    e. The migratory bird rule, concerning what could be regulated as wetlands

10. The Clean Air Act of 1990
    a. established tighter standards for emissions of nitrogen dioxide from cars and trucks.
    b. forced 110 coal-burning power plants to shut down.
    c. required Los Angeles to reduce its air pollution more quickly than other cities.
    d. required that CFC production cease immediately.
    e. passed with very little lobbying.

11. The Kyoto Protocol was rejected by the U.S. Senate because
    a. there is no global warming.
    b. it is not cost effective to solve the problem with today's technology.
    c. European countries have not signed on.
    d. it lacks the support of the United Nations.
    e. developing nations that signed on faced only voluntary limits to their emissions.

12. To pay for a budget deficit, the federal government
    a. usually sells off public land holdings.
    b. almost always increases taxes.
    c. issues U.S. Treasury bonds.
    d. increases the amount of money in circulation.
    e. will borrow money from other nations.

13. Monetary policy is primarily made by
    a. the president.
    b. Congress.
    c. the Federal Reserve.
    d. the treasury secretary.
    e. the federal mint.

14. Under a regressive tax proposal,
    a. people with high incomes pay a lower percentage in taxes than people with low incomes.
    b. people pay according to their ability to pay.
    c. prior progressive taxes are repealed.
    d. the national debt goes up.
    e. people with low incomes pay a lower percentage in taxes than people with high incomes.

15. Which of the following taxes is not a regressive tax?
    a. the Federal income tax
    b. the Social Security tax
    c. a state sales tax
    d. local real estate taxes
    e. the Medicare tax

16. The only major industrialized nation with a lower total amount of taxes collected than the U.S. is
    a. Sweden.
    b. Germany.
    c. Great Britain.
    d. Spain.
    e. Japan.

17. Legal methods in the tax code of avoiding taxes are referred to as
    a. justifications.
    b. hidden benefits.
    c. loopholes.
    d. give-backs.
    e. regressive taxes.

18. The Social Security system is in crisis because
    a. the pension fund lost money in the stock market.
    b. too much money has been allotted for homeland security.
    c. people receiving benefits are greedy.
    d. the government didn't budget enough money for the program.
    e. the large number of baby boomers will retire, and fewer workers will pay for the program.

19. The level of U.S. imports compared to other countries is
    a. one of the highest in the world.
    b. unusually large for a developed nation.
    c. smack dab in the middle.
    d. relatively small.
    e. indeterminate because of globalization and security.

20. A major concern about the World Trade Organization is that it will
    a. strengthen multi-national corporations.
    b. eliminate unionization of workers in developing nations.
    c. increase tariffs on goods from nonmember countries.
    d. lack the power to actually regulate trade.
    e. weaken environmental, health, and safety laws.

Short Essay   Briefly address the major concepts raised by the following questions.

1. Explain and discuss the steps in the policymaking process.

2. Analyze the major issues of crime in the United States.

3. Discuss the major laws that aim to protect the nation's environment.

4. Explain the issues related to Social Security.

ANSWERS TO THE PRACTICE EXAM

Fill-in-the-Blank
1. domestic policy
2. policy adoption
3. income transfers
4. juveniles
5. drug offenses
6. National Environmental Policy Act
7. global warming
8. Keynesian economics

9. working, retired
10. World Trade Organization

True/False

1. T	3. F	5. T	7. T	9. T
2. T	4. F	6. F	8. F	10. T

Multiple Choice

1. c	5. b	9. e	13. c	17. c
2. b	6. b	10. a	14. a	18. e
3. b	7. e	11. e	15. a	19. d
4. b	8. a	12. c	16. e	20. e

Short Essay

1. Explain and discuss the steps in the policymaking process.

The policymaking process consists of five major steps: 1)agenda building, 2) policy formulation, 3) policy adoption, 4) policy implementation, and 5) policy evaluation

Agenda building is the first step. The media, strong personalities, and interest groups usually facilitate this recognition of the problem.

Policy formulation is the discussion between the government and the public of various proposals to solve the problem.

Policy adoption is the selection by Congress of a specific strategy from the proposals discussed.

Policy implementation is the government action implemented by bureaucrats, the courts, the police, and individual citizens.

Policy evaluation is groups inside and outside receiving feedback about the policy and planning changes or improvements.

2. Analyze the major issues of crime in the United States.
   - Crime has been an American concern since the days of the American Revolution.
   - Two trends that concern Americans are violent crime and serious crimes committed by juveniles.
   - Violent crime dropped steadily from the mid-1990s to today. (See Figure 14-6.)
   - Homicide rates shot up from 1960 to 1980 but have lately dropped. (See Figure 14-7.)
   - Theft rates have experienced a steady decline from 1970 onward. (See Figure 14-8.)
   - Juvenile crime rose from the late 1980s to about 1995. (See Figure 14-9.)
   - School shootings are high-profile crimes that have become alarmingly common at every level of education.
   - The United States has the highest incarceration rate of any country in the world. (See Figure 14-10.)
   - Not all groups of Americans are incarcerated at the same rates: men more than women, African Americans more than anybody else. (See Table 14-1.)
   - These incarceration rates have a tremendous impact on prisoners' families, and specifically their children.
   - A major cause of incarceration in America is illegal drug offenses. Alternative ways to address drug use have been proposed and put into practice by states but not on the federal level.
   - Terrorism has become a newly devastating crime concern of Americans.

3. Discuss the major laws that aim to protect the nation's environment.

Government legislation to control pollution can be traced back to before the American Revolution. The most concerted effort to clean up the environment began in 1969 with the passage of the National Environmental Policy Act. This law required that an environmental impact statement (EIS) be prepared for all major federal actions that might impact the environment.

The 1990 Clean Air Act was designed to clean up air pollution by regulating vehicle emissions and coal plant emissions and by calling for the elimination of chlorofluorocarbons.

The Clean Water Act of 1972 established the following three goals: to make waters safe for swimming, to protect fish and wildlife, and to eliminate the discharge of pollutants. There has been controversy over the part of the act that applies to wetlands.

Global warming has been another controversial issue, with debate over the extent of its impact as well as, from some researchers, its general veracity.

The Kyoto Protocol has been ratified by 124 countries, but the Senate refused to recognize it in 1997, due to the fact that developing countries could sign on but face only voluntary limits to their emissions.

In 2007, the EPA was forced by the Supreme Court to regulate greenhouse gasses and, specifically, carbon dioxide emissions.

4. Explain the issues related to Social Security.
    *   The viability of the Social Security system is an issue concerning more and more individuals, because most Americans will age.
    *   The system now is a pay-as-you-go transfer system in which those who are working are paying benefits to those who are retired.
    *   Today there are about three workers to provide for each retiree's Social Security and Medicare. With the imminent retirement of a huge group of baby boomers, the ratio will drop to two workers in 2030. (See Figure 14-13.)
    *   A variety of solutions have been proposed, such as raising the Social Security payroll tax, eliminating the current cap on the level of wages to tax, increasing the age to receive full benefits to 70, and allowing immigrants to qualify for benefits (and therefore pay into the system).
    *   In 2004, President Bush proposed the privatization of the system to allow individuals to invest in the financial markets. This reform measure faced harsh criticism that eliminated its chances of passage.

Chapter 15
FOREIGN POLICY

CHAPTER SUMMARY

On September 11, 2001—overnight—Americans faced profound changes in their view of national security and foreign policy. What tools does our government have as it tackles these issues, both at home and abroad?

Facing the World: Foreign and Defense Policy

Foreign policy is the term used to describe a nation's external goals and the techniques and strategies used to achieve them. These techniques can include diplomacy, economic aid, technical assistance, or military intervention. Two key aspects of foreign policy are national security, the protection of the independence and political integrity of the United States (including defense policy), and diplomacy, the settlement of disputes and conflicts among nations by peaceful methods.

Morality versus Reality in Foreign Policy

From the early days of the United States, many American policymakers have felt an obligation to provide moral leadership to the rest of the world. Many U.S. foreign policy initiatives seem to be rooted in moral idealism, a philosophy that sees all nations as willing to cooperate and agree on moral standards for conduct. In opposition to the moral perspective is political realism, a philosophy that sees the world as a dangerous place in which each nation strives for its own survival. The United States has generally pursued a foreign policy that attempts to balance these philosophies. Since 2001, the War on Terror has tested the United States commitment to international cooperation.

Challenges in World Politics

In a new development, dissident groups, rebels, and other revolutionaries have used modern weapons to engage in terrorism in order to affect world politics. The long-standing regional conflict in the Middle East has produced a number of terrorist acts both regionally and worldwide in the last two decades. In 2001, terrorism reached the United States with the attacks on the World Trade Center and Pentagon. In response, the George W. Bush administration embarked on its "war on terrorism," which entailed military efforts in Afghanistan and Iraq and represents a new U.S. doctrine of preemptive attack. Iraq has been a repeated target of U.S. military action, first when it occupied Kuwait in 1991 (by the George H.W. Bush administration) and again in 2003 as part of the George W. Bush doctrine of unilateral preemption. The second gulf war did succeed in toppling the Hussein regime, but further occupation of the country has proven very trying for both the U.S. military and the citizens of Iraq. (See Figure 15-1 for a look at the ethno-religious groups in Iraq.) The spring of 2004 marked a major downturn in the war, with Sunnis fighting Shiites, both fighting the occupation forces, the military scandal at Abu Ghraib, and public support in the U.S. on the wane. As of 2006, two-thirds of Americans polled said they would like to see an end to the war. A 2007 poll of Iraqis reveals that 78% are opposed to the U.S. occupation. In January 2007, President Bush announced a "surge" of troops in an effort to bring the insurgency to an end. This, in combination with tribal leaders shifting their alliances to the U.S., has led to a relatively stable Iraq. In addition to the war in Iraq, issues of nuclear weaponry and nuclear proliferation are still major policy subjects. The dissolution of the Soviet Union brought a lowering of tensions among the nuclear powers, but the number and location of nuclear weapons continue to be major problems. Additionally, more nations are developing—or are thought to be able to develop—nuclear weapons, notably India and Pakistan, Iran, and North Korea. North Korea appears to be willing to negotiate about their nuclear weapons factories in exchange for foreign aid. China poses new challenges in world politics, with its Communist government, world's largest population, and position as a major U.S. trading partner. It is expected that the U.S. will no longer be the sole superpower and China will fill the power vacuum left by the Soviet Union. Other sites of regional conflict include Cuba, many nations in Africa, Darfur specifically, and Israel and Palestine. Cuba has been a long-term source of tension for U.S. administrations. Africa faces challenges from AIDS and from massive ethnic and civil wars in countries including Angola, Rwanda, and Sudan; the U.S. has been slow to intervene in all of these conflicts. In 2007, Sudan announced it would accept United Nations Peacekeepers to help end the genocide in Darfur. Clashes between Israel and its Arab neighbors have been a concern of the United States since the conflict began in 1948. As recently as the summer 2006, violence continued to erupt, as Israel went to war with the militant group Hezbollah in Lebanon.

Who Makes Foreign Policy?

The president is given broad constitutional powers over foreign policy, though Congress also has policymaking responsibilities; the branches often act jointly or, sometimes, in conflict. The two most significant presidential powers are the leadership of the armed forces as commander-in-chief and the negotiation of treaties and executive agreements. The president also appoints ambassadors and consuls and can recognize other nations by receiving their ambassadors. There are also many informal sources of presidential foreign policy powers that stem from precedent and the president's personality. With great access to information, the president can act quickly to influence fund allocation or the moral or political course of the nation. Presidents also have great sway over public opinion. In addition to the president, there are four foreign policymaking sources within the executive branch. First, the Department of State is the department most directly engaged in day-to-day foreign policy, but this department can possess more negative constituents than positive domestic supporters. Next, the National Security Council is responsible for advising the president on domestic, foreign, and military policies affecting national security. This council is used in different ways by different presidents. Third is the intelligence community, which is composed of all government agencies involved in intelligence activities and includes the CIA (the key member), the NSA, the DIA, the FBI, and the military intelligence agencies. Their actions can be overt or covert; the latter have caused controversy upon discovery. The Internet has dramatically changed intelligence gathering and methods. Finally, the Department of Defense brings all military agencies under one organization headed by a civilian secretary of defense.

Congress Balances the Presidency

The struggle between the president and Congress over foreign policy questions reached a high point during the Vietnam War (1964-1975). In 1973, Congress passed, over President's Nixon's veto, the War Powers Resolution, which required the president to consult Congress before using troops in military action. In reality, most presidents have not consulted Congress in this manner. Congress also possesses the Power of the Purse where it can limit or refuse presidential requests for funding that would go to certain groups or programs. Congress' ability to limit funding is a precarious weapon as illustrated with Iraq war funding bills. If members pass the war funding, they fail to fulfill their campaign promises to end the war. If they refuse to fund the war, they are abandoning the soldiers in the field.

The Major Foreign Policy Themes

A historical review of American foreign policy reveals several major themes. In the early days of our nation, the founding fathers held a basic mistrust of alliances with European nations. The Monroe Doctrine of 1823 warned European nations not to become involved in the affairs of nations in the Western Hemisphere. The Monroe Doctrine also set forth a U.S. policy of isolationism toward Europe, a policy characterized by abstaining from an active role in international affairs or alliances, particularly with Europe. The end of the isolationist policy started with the Spanish-American War in 1898 and continued with American involvement in World War I (1914-1918). After World War I, America returned briefly to a policy of isolationism that ended dramatically with the Japanese bombing of Pearl Harbor on December 7, 1941, prompting U.S. entry into World War II. The United States embarked upon a policy of internationalism that would continue for the remainder of the century. The WWII alliance between the U.S. and the Soviet Union was fragile and quickly developed into the fifty-year struggle of the Cold War. The Soviet Union seized parts of Eastern Europe and divided the continent with what Winston Churchill called an "iron curtain." In response, the U.S. adopted a policy of containment, the Truman Doctrine, and entered into a number of military alliances designed to prevent the spread of Communism. (See Figure 15-2 for a look at Europe during the Cold War.) The military alliances were tested in a series of military actions, usually by "client" nations of each side. In the Korean War (1950-1953) and the Vietnam War (1964-1975), the United States engaged directly in military action against forces supported by Communist regimes. The Cuban Missile Crisis in 1962 brought the world to the brink of nuclear war, but after this crisis was peacefully resolved, the United States and the Soviet Union entered a period of relaxed tension known as détente. The Strategic

Arms Limitation Treaty (SALT I) of the Nixon administration began a process of reducing nuclear weapons, but in the 1980s President Reagan took a harder line with the Soviet Union, recalling the early days of the Cold War. In 1985, however, Reagan and Mikhail Gorbachev began negotiations for what would become the Intermediate-Range Nuclear Force (INF) Treaty of 1987. President George H.W. Bush continued arms reduction negotiations, including signing the Strategic Arms Reduction Treaty (START) in 1992. The Soviet Union, faced with growing internal unrest (exemplified by the dramatic fall of the Berlin Wall), officially dissolved on December 26, 1991. (See Figure 15-3 for a look at Europe after the fall of the Soviet Union.) In recent years, a resurgent and much more assertive Russia, has emerged under the leadership of former President and current Prime Minister Putin. In support of pro-Moscow separatists, Putin ordered the invasion of Georgia, a former Soviet Republic. Despite tremendous international condemnation, the Russian military continues to occupy the separatist regions. The future relationship between Russia and its neighbors is of great international concern.

KEY TERMS

Cold War
containment
defense policy
détente
diplomacy
economic aid
foreign policy
foreign policy process
intelligence community
iron curtain
isolationist foreign policy

Monroe Doctrine
moral idealism
national security policy
negative constituents
normal trade relations (NTR) status
political realism
Soviet bloc
Strategic Arms Limitation Treaty (SALT I)
technical assistance
Truman Doctrine

OTHER RESOURCES

A number of valuable supplements are available to students using the Schmidt, Shelley, and Bardes text. A list of suggested supplements is at the end of the chapter. Ask your instructor how to obtain these resources. One supplement is highlighted here, The Freedom House.

E-MOCRACY EXERCISES

Direct URL: http://www.freedomhouse.org/template.cfm?page=363&year=2008

Surfing Instructions:
Log on to www.freedomhouse.org
In the upper right hand corner, click on "Map of Freedom."
In the drop-down choice select the map from year 2005 and compare it to the map from 2008.

Study Questions
1. From 2005 to 2008, did the world's net freedom increase or decrease?
2. Upon which continent is the largest number "not free" or "partly free."
3. What are some of the problems that Freedom House identified in the United States?

PRACTICE EXAM

(Answers appear at the end of this chapter.)

Fill-in-the-Blank   Supply the missing word(s) or term(s) to complete the sentence.

1. _____ _____ describes U.S. goals, techniques, and strategies in the world arena.

2. _____ refers to the peaceful settlement of disputes and conflicts among nations.

3. The _____ _____ is the department most directly engaged in foreign affairs.

4. The _____ _____ formed the basis for the U.S. foreign policy of isolationism.

5. The lasting change in American foreign policy came with the end of _____ _____ _____.

6. The doctrine created by George F. Kennan, which became the driving force of western foreign policy, was _____.

7. President Eisenhower warned the nation about the influence of the _____-_____ _____.

8. The French word that means a relaxation of tensions is _____.

9. In 2006 Israel waged war with the militant group _____ in Lebanon.

10. The fall of the Berlin Wall signaled the beginning of the dissolution of the _____ _____.

True/False   Circle the appropriate letter to indicate if the statement is true or false.

T   F   1. National security policy concerns itself with the defense of the U.S. against actual or potential enemies.

T   F   2. Diplomacy is the set of negotiation techniques by which the U.S. attempts to carry out its foreign policy.

T   F   3. The Peace Corps is a good example of America's moral idealism in practice.

T   F   4. Political realism has always been the only guiding principle in foreign policy decisions for the U.S.

T   F   5. China has become a major trading partner of the United States.

T   F   6. The State Department's preeminence in foreign policy has gradually increased since WWII.

T   F   7. The country of Russia is no longer a foreign policy threat to the United States.

T   F   8. U.S. foreign policy during its formative years could be described as interventionist.

T   F   9. The Star Wars policy of President Clinton brought an end to the Communist threat.

T   F   10. The Truman Doctrine is a clear expression of the U.S. policy of containment.

Multiple-Choice   Circle the correct response.

1.   Diplomacy differs from national security policy in that
    a.   diplomacy is a process to settle conflicts among nations by peaceful means.
    b.   diplomacy is the all-encompassing goal, while national security policy is a sub-set of tactics.
    c.   the president develops diplomacy and the State Department develops national security policy.
    d.   diplomacy always comes first, followed by a specific national security policy.
    e.   diplomacy always makes use of the United Nations.

2.   The foreign policy that allows the U.S. to sell weapons to dictators who support American business interests around the world and to repel terrorism with force is the policy of
    a.   détente.
    b.   moral idealism.
    c.   counterintelligence.
    d.   political realism.
    e.   economic materialism.

3.   The concept of "preemptive war" as a defense strategy is
    a.   based on World War II experiences.
    b.   based on Cold War experiences.
    c.   not part of United States foreign policy.
    d.   known as the Clinton doctrine.
    e.   known as the Bush doctrine.

4.   Concern over nuclear weapon proliferation intensified in 1999 when the Senate rejected the
    a.   China/North Korea Treaty.
    b.   Comprehensive Nuclear Test Ban Treaty.
    c.   Middle East Peace Treaty.
    d.   Nuclear Terrorism Treaty.
    e.   India/Pakistan Treaty

5.   Relations between the U.S. and Cuba are still politically important because of
    a.   NAFTA.
    b.   Raul Castro's democratic leanings.
    c.   the Cuban-American voter bloc in Florida.
    d.   the Cuban government's oversight of Guantanamo Naval Base.
    e.   the attack of Cuban terrorists in New York.

6.   One of the major problems in Africa is the
    a.   spread of nuclear weapons.
    b.   spread of Communism.
    c.   government of Saddam Hussein.
    d.   AIDS epidemic.
    e.   weapons of mass destruction in the Sudan.

7.   The major provision of the War Powers Act was to
    a.   limit the president's use of troops in military action without congressional approval.
    b.   allow the president more freedom in the use of military troops throughout the world.
    c.   give the president new powers in the area of foreign policy.
    d.   prevent aggressor nations from becoming too strong militarily.
    e.   establish the "preemptive war" concept.

8. The making of foreign policy is often viewed as a presidential prerogative because
   a. most presidents enjoy making foreign policy.
   b. of the president's constitutional power in this area and the resources of the executive branch.
   c. the Constitution clearly denies Congress a role in formulating foreign policy.
   d. the War Powers Act delegated this authority to the president.
   e. of the numbers of wars presidents have declared over the years.

9. Which of the following is **not** an informal power of the president to influence foreign policy?
   a. The ability to gain access to information and intelligence
   b. The ability to influence public opinion
   c. The ability to influence government spending
   d. The ability to provide moral leadership
   e. The ability to recognize foreign governments

10. The role of the National Security Council is to
    a. shape executive agreements for the president.
    b. protect the president overseas.
    c. advise the president on the integration of policies relating to national security.
    d. supervise the CIA.
    e. coordinate the war on terror.

11. The international perspective that views the world as a dangerous place in which each nation strives for its own survival and interests regardless of other considerations is a good definition for which term?
    a. zealots.
    b. Neo-conservativism
    c. political realism
    d. Bush Doctrine
    e. moral idealism

12. The president who warned the nation of the influence of the military-industrial complex was
    a. Eisenhower.
    b. Nixon.
    c. Reagan.
    d. Clinton.
    e. George W. Bush.

13. The Monroe Doctrine states that the U.S.
    a. had territorial dominion over South America.
    b. was neutral in its relations with Europe and Asia.
    c. could trade openly with China.
    d. would not meddle in European internal affairs and would not accept foreign intervention in the Western Hemisphere.
    e. would not allow weapons of mass destruction in the Western Hemisphere.

14. The event that signified the Soviet Union had relinquished its political and military control over the states of Eastern Europe was
    a. its renewed interest in Cuba.
    b. the fall of the Berlin Wall.
    c. its defeat in Afghanistan.
    d. the dissolution of Yugoslavia.
    e. the Warsaw Pact.

15. The strategic defense initiative (SDI or "Star Wars") was proposed as a program that would deter nuclear war by
    a. shifting the emphasis of defense strategy from offensive to defensive weapons systems.
    b. shifting our defense to an offensive weapons system.
    c. developing more intercontinental ballistic missiles.
    d. allowing for joint United States/Soviet Union development of manned space stations with laser-guided missiles for world domination.
    e. eliminating the axis of evil.

16. The START treaty
    a. allowed Russia to join NATO.
    b. reduced the number of long-range nuclear weapons.
    c. gave China most-favored-nation status.
    d. created the "Star Wars" initiative.
    e. gave the United Nations authority over Iraq.

17. The phrase "iron curtain" was coined by
    a. Ronald Reagan.
    b. Franklin Roosevelt.
    c. John Kennedy.
    d. Joseph Stalin.
    e. Winston Churchill.

18. The Cold War
    a. featured direct clashes between the U.S. and the U.S.S.R.
    b. was fought mainly between "client" nations.
    c. was so named because of the icy diplomatic relations between combatants.
    d. includes the First Gulf War.
    e. ended with the 1973 peace agreement in Vietnam.

19. Operation Desert Storm, carried out by the U.S. and a coalition of other nations, led to the
    a. overthrow of Saddam Hussein in Iraq.
    b. overthrow of the Sheikdom of Kuwait.
    c. restoration of the Sheikdom of Kuwait.
    d. overthrow of the government in Iran.
    e. overthrow of the government in Saudi Arabia.

20. The Second Gulf War had the stated goal of
    a. overthrowing Saddam Hussein in Iraq.
    b. overthrowing Fidel Castro in Cuba.
    c. overthrowing the Taliban in Afghanistan.
    d. seizing weapons of mass destruction in Iran.
    e. securing oil supplies for the United States in Iraq.

Short Essay   Briefly address the major concepts raised by the following questions.

1. Trace the United States' foreign policy efforts to fight terrorism.

2. Describe the formal and informal powers of the president to make foreign policy.

3. Discuss the current foreign policy challenges the U.S. faces, other than regional conflicts.

4. Summarize the role that the U.S. has played in recent regional conflicts.

5. Trace the stages of United States foreign policy development from isolationism through détente.

ANSWERS TO THE PRACTICE EXAM

Fill-in-the-Blank
1. Foreign policy
2. Diplomacy
3. State Department
4. Monroe Doctrine
5. World War II
6. containment
7. military-industrial complex
8. détente
9. Hezbollah
10. Soviet Union

True/False

1. T	3. T	5. T	7. F	9. F
2. T	4. F	6. F	8. F	10. T

Multiple Choice

1. a	5. c	9. e	13. d	17. e
2. d	6. d	10. c	14. b	18. b
3. e	7. a	11. c	15. a	19. c
4. b	8. b	12. a	16. b	20. a

Short Essay   An adequate short answer consists of several paragraphs that discuss the concepts addressed by the question. Always demonstrate your knowledge of the ideas by giving examples. The following represent the major ideas that should be included in these short essays.

1. Trace the United States' foreign policy efforts to fight terrorism.
   - The first military response to 9/11 by the U.S was directed against al Qaeda camps in Afghanistan and led to the overthrow of the Taliban government in Afghanistan.
   - In 2002, President Bush issued the "Bush Doctrine" of "preemptive war" to fight terrorism.
   - Two Presidents Bush have led the U.S. into two Gulf Wars. The first was intended to force Iraq to withdraw from Kuwait. The second was intended to topple Saddam Hussein and ultimately involved the occupation of the nation of Iraq.
   - The extreme lack of security in Iraq today threatens the U.S. plan to reduce terrorism by installing a democracy in Iraq.
   - Two-thirds of Americans want the war to end and 78% of Iraqis are against the U.S. occupation.

2. Describe the formal and informal powers of the president to make foreign policy.
The Constitution provides the president with these areas of foreign policy authority:
Article II, Section 1 designates the president as commander-in-chief of the armed forces.
Article II, Section 2 gives the president the power to make treaties (with the consent of two-thirds of the Senate). Additional foreign policy power is granted to appoint ambassadors, other public ministers, and consuls. Section 3 gives the president the power to recognize foreign governments.
The informal powers of the president to conduct foreign policy include the superior access to information, the ability to lobby Congress for funds, influence over public opinion, and the head-of-state moral leadership position for committing the U.S. to a course of action.

3. Discuss the current foreign policy challenges the U.S. faces, other than regional conflicts.
Nuclear proliferation remains a world problem as more nations, including the unpredictable North Korea and Iran, join the "Nuclear Club."

President Nixon was responsible for opening diplomatic and economic relations with China in the 1970s. China became a major trading partner of the United States in the 1990s. China sought and received most-favored-nation status (now called normal trade relations status) for tariffs and trade policy from the United States.

4. Summarize the role that the U.S. has played in recent regional conflicts.

Cuba continues to influence American policymaking because of the large Cuban-American immigrant population in the election-important state of Florida.

The Middle East crisis between Israel and its Arab neighbors has been a long-standing regional conflict. The United States has repeatedly tried and failed to bring about a peaceful settlement of the conflict.

The invasion of Kuwait by Iraq in 1990 created an additional Middle East crisis for the U.S. In Operation Desert Storm, the United States, with a coalition of nations under United Nations authority, pushed Iraq out of Kuwait. Iraq, under United Nations sanctions, has continued to defy the world and has created an environment of regional tension.

Ethnic conflicts have broken out in a number of African nations. The conflicts have been made more devastating because of drought, AIDS, and famine conditions in many countries. The often untimely efforts of the United Nations and United States have been unable to stop the conflicts.

In 2007, the president of Sudan relented and is permitting UN peacekeepers (with U.S. advisors) to help end the genocide in Darfur.

5. Trace the stages of United States foreign policy development from isolationism through détente.

The founders of the United States distrusted the European nations and attempted to stay out of European conflicts and politics. This policy of isolation from Europe was stated in the Monroe Doctrine in 1823.

The end of the isolationist policy started with the Spanish-American War in 1898. It continued to change in World War I when the United States intervened in a European conflict.

Isolation returned after World War I in reaction to that conflict.

Isolation ended forever on December 7, 1941, when the Japanese attacked Pearl Harbor and the United States was thrust into World War II. The era of internationalism had begun.

Although the United States and the Soviet Union were wartime allies against Nazi Germany, the alliance quickly fell apart after the war. The Soviet Union wanted a divided Germany and seized control of Eastern Europe to create a Soviet Bloc, which would challenge the Western world in an ideological, political, and economic struggle known as the Cold War.

The United States foreign policy throughout the Cold War was the "containment" of the spread of Communism. This was laid out in the Truman Doctrine.

In the Cuban Missile Crisis of 1962, the United States and the Soviet Union confronted each other over the placement of Soviet missiles in Cuba. This crisis led the world to the brink of a nuclear war. After intense negotiations, the crisis was resolved in a peaceful manner.

After the Cuban Missile Crisis, the United States and the Soviet Union realized that they had to reduce the threat of nuclear war. Under the leadership of President Nixon and Henry Kissinger, a period of détente, or relaxation of tensions, began. The first tangible result of détente was the Strategic Arms Limitation Treaty (SALT I) signed in 1972.